Wandering Lonely in a Crowd

Reflections on the Muslim Condition in the West

S. M. Atif Imtiaz

KUBE
PUBLISHING

First published in England by Kube Publishing Ltd.,
Markfield Conference Centre
Ratby Lane, Markfield,
Leicestershire LE67 9SY
United Kingdom
Tel: +44 (0) 1530 249230
Fax: +44 (0) 1530 249656
Website: www.kubepublishing.com
Email: info@kubepublishing.com

A Cataloguing-in-Publication data record is
available from the British Library.

ISBN 978-1-84774-024-3 *paperback*

Typesetting: Naiem Qaddoura
Cover Design: Inspiral Design Ltd.

Contents

Foreword

Despite all the raucous debate about Islam in Britain and British Muslims in the last decade, there has been far too little sustained reflection of real insight. Here is a precious sample of such reflection from Atif Imtiaz, whose combination of intellectualism and vivid reportage makes for a compelling mix. Who else would be reading Camus and Nietzsche on his way to the anti-war demonstrations in London from Bradford? He has an ear for the nuance of conversation and then applies a razor-like analysis to pick apart how people speak and what they are saying or would like to say.

Camus is not the only surprise in here. There are plenty more unpredictable juxtapositions. Indeed, the very structure of the book offers exactly that; the contrasts between styles of writing draw out the loose threads. Imtiaz, thank goodness, is not satisfied with easy conclusions. So we are offered a rich mix of ideas, influences, and people rather than neat ideology or argument. It provides a much better glimpse of the difficulties and confusions that Imtiaz – and many others of his generation and background – have had to navigate over the last 15 years.

From student radicalism in the nineties to being at the centre of national security in the 2000s, Imtiaz's generation of British Muslims have had to confront issues of identity, belonging, loyalty, commitment and their faith in much harsher and more polarised terms than most. Nor does that journey seem to be over – Imtiaz offers a way into the conversation rather than a destination. At its best, *Wandering Lonely in a Crowd* reads like eavesdropping in on a community which has too often been misrepresented, simplified and even, on occasion, demonised.

A careful thinker, drawing inspiration from many different sources including, of course, his Islamic faith, Imtiaz is one of those who is exploring and articulating what a twenty-first century Western expression of his religion might mean.

Madeleine Bunting
London
April 2010

Introduction: Every Text has its Context

His violence precedes his presence, to the eye at least. A shot rings out across the red, open desert. His bullet arrives before he does. But from where, the eye cannot tell. We know nothing of him, but we know his bullet. It has killed Lawrence's guide as he drank from a well. He rides in, off the desert, and a speck on the horizon becomes a horse, a man riding a horse, an Arab. He descends from his horse, removes his scarf and we are introduced to Sherif Ali who will become Lawrence's closest aide and companion throughout the rest of his adventures in David Lean's *Lawrence of Arabia*.

The vague, the blurred, the background, the speck on the horizon, the almost irrelevant has assumed centre stage. What was previously the concern of a minority of academics and even fewer funding bodies has now become one of the most serious and crucial issues of our times. The consequences of this scrutiny remain unclear. As Geertz (2003) has highlighted in his review of some of the literature post-11th September:

> What isn't clear, and will not become so for quite some time, is where it all is taking us, what our sense of this obscure and threatening Other that has appeared suddenly – and literally – on our domestic horizon is going ultimately to be.[1]

So what is the focus of this book? It is to collect together a series of essays, short stories and speeches on two debates that focus on the Muslim community in Britain: the terrorism debate and the integration debate. Both debates have assumed prime political importance since 2001 due to the riots that took place in Oldham, Burnley and Bradford in the summer of that year and the terrorist attacks in New York and Washington. Before I proceed to introduce and describe the chapters of this book I would like to introduce my perspective on the context.

To paraphrase Denise Jodelet, a transformation in immigration policy swings open the doors of a country, and the social situation which emerges overturns mental attitudes whose roots are to be found in the distant past.[2] That is, that mass migration in the post-war period resulted in the transformation of 'otherness' from an exogenous to an endogenous form. This act of economic migration unleashes a social process that is as complex as it is deep in its constitutive structure. It is deep because it draws upon a history of a thousand years which includes West–Muslim interactions such as the Crusades, Andalusia, the Mughal Empire and the Raj, the Ottoman Empire and colonialism. It is complex because it involves three types of 'otherness' – race, culture and religion – which are themselves differentially received. The contradictory nature of the legal and psychological denial of racism (namely that criminalizing racism can lead to a backlash in society in support of racism), the problem of incorporating a tolerant attitude towards cultures (this being at a time of rapid transformation of culture itself), and the vexed approach to religion *per se* and Islam in particular, all serve to complicate the picture. The maturing of the second generation of South Asian Muslims through the British educational system and under the umbrella of liberal ideology would raise the issues of 'otherness' that might have otherwise remained in the background. What does it mean to be represented as 'other'? What are the effects of such a representation on identity? What should be left in the past, and what ought to be carried into the future? How does British society respond to the endogenisation of 'otherness'? And how would the second generation respond to British society's response to the endogenisation of 'otherness'?

The constant pulling and pushing, 'You are different to us!', 'We are the same as you!', the oscillation between the exacerbation and the reduction of difference – the dialectics of the endogenisation of 'otherness' – and the consequences of this upon those who are represented as 'other', these are the themes that I will attempt to explore throughout this book.

How to understand Islam? It is Oriental, yet it is also Occidental. It is past, yet present. It refuses categorization: the nearest of the Eastern religions and the most modern of the old religions: it questions our assumptions. Though its origin in time and place is far, it draws near enough to confound the 'otherness' that is placed upon it. If it is 'other', it is not completely so. This, however, has not prevented a historical proliferation of stereotypes of the Islamic world as attempts to pin down this denier of categories.

Charles Husband suggested, for example, that: 'historically derived stereotypes of Islam and 'the Orient' are continuously latent within British popular culture and learning'.[3] Bipolar juxtapositioning seems to be a familiar theme and a series of researchers have pointed to the bipolar nature of this relationship. For example, William Watt as a major authority on Christian-Muslim relations summarised twelfth- and thirteenth-century Christian views of Islam as violent and sexually indulgent in contrast to Christian self-images of the time.[4] Edward Said provided the example of British and French Orientalism which made Islam 'Other' for the purposes of empire.[5] He offered the example of Lord Cromer's juxtaposition of the rational, logical, evidence-requiring European against the irrational, self-contradictory and opaque Oriental. The extent to which these stereotypes are embedded within European intellectual history has been highlighted by Alain Grosrichard who examined, through Lacanian analysis, the interpretation of the Ottoman Caliphate as despotic by Montesquieu in contradiction to the emerging (European) rational society through, for example, depictions of the harem and the seraglio.[6] Dolar writes in the introduction:

It is the time of spectacular endeavours proposing a rationally based society, a new concept of state, civil society, democratic liberties, citizenship, division of power, and so on; but in a strange counterpoint, there was the image of Oriental despotism as the very negative of those endeavours, their phantasmic Other.[7]

To continue this theme, Bryan Turner, a leading authority on Weber, concludes after examining Weber's sociology of oriental society that 'the Orient simply lacks the positive ingredients of Western rationality. Oriental society can be defined as a system of absences....'[8] Even in terms of projecting a future identity for Europe, Kathryn Woodward has noted that a resurgent European identity has 'been produced against the threat of 'the Other'. This 'Other' often includes workers from North Africa... who are construed as representing a threat from Islamic fundamentalism'.[9] Mohja Kahf has written on the history of the depiction of Muslim women and contrasts between two main templates: the turgomen and the odalisque, the first to have been historically superseded by the second.[10] The turgomen was the Eastern queen: intelligent, beautiful and powerful. The odalisque was the subjugated victim. That both have functioned as representations casts doubt upon a linear, monolithic narrative but one wonders how both representations reflected the position of women in European society. In my own research on Bradford Muslims and the Rushdie Affair, I contrasted the stereotype of the Muslim during the Rushdie Affair as violent, ignorant, illiterate and hypocritical with its opposite – the liberal individual – as humane, educated, literate and genuine.[11] It is difficult to employ abstractions, such as a self/other mutually antagonistic bifurcation, or indeed any abstractions in order to explain a relationship that has lasted for over a thousand years, across several continents but there nevertheless have been instances in the history of the cultural representation of Islam and Muslims when the central explanation has been negatively-evaluated sheer difference.[12] Unfortunately, it seems at present as if we are living through a time in which this theme of difference – worryingly irreconcilable difference – is constantly being offered as an explanation for the actions of others. The argument moves from referring to individual cases to lists of examples to wholesale theories – it is a construction of a narrative that is constantly being attempted at a time of great change. Another major aspect of the context of these debates is the great social change that has occurred in Western society in general but in British society in particular. This social change could be termed the rise of excessive individualism, detraditionalisation, demoralisation or the 'hollowing out' of modern society.[13] It is an argument about how freedom has perhaps been taken too far, such that society itself is threatened and as such it is an argument that strikes at the psychological core of British society because there is no greater defining aspect of the modern British state than its reverence for freedom. But the debate about detraditionalisation or social evils calls into question the prime importance attributed to the value of freedom. It asks whether there is enough within the values and structures of a bureaucratised, meritocratic state to propel society as a whole towards a quality of life for its citizens that is acceptable and satisfying.[14] The intellectuals and policy wonks involved in this debate are loathe to frame the debate in any manner which would encourage the return of religion (it was after all Durkheim as a founding father of sociology who warned against the excesses of individualism) and yet in many British cities there are now communities emerging that – though they may have similarly been affected by the atmosphere of liberation that surrounds them – present as real life alternatives to the problems of excessive individualism. They call for community and discipline but this also creates an anxiety around the return of authoritarianism – and so the excessive communalism of these communities is criticised. This context that Islam in particular and religion in general may be a meaningful and practical response to excessive individualism also affects the terms, the style and the manner of the discussions that surround the community.

Another major aspect to the context that presents itself to British society is recent international political history. Modernisation in the Muslim world has been a difficult process and it is only now that Muslim modernities are beginning to emerge. If the initial supposition was that Muslim modernity was oxymoronic and the rise of Islamic movements was the concomitant outcome, the present debate is more about what a Muslim modernity looks like whether this be in relation to city planning, education or public health. But the stresses that were created in a post-war nation-state settlement across the Muslim world are only now after the demise of the Cold War being dealt with and this has meant that feudalism and various kingships as well as the positioning of borders have been challenged. The political uncertainty that this has generated has placed Muslim communities in the West in the difficult situation where they have felt obliged to speak out against policies of their governments which have ranged from direct intervention to passive acquiescence. If the transformation of immigration policy, the cultural history of representation, the intellectual-social context of a society in flux and international politics have all served to render the unfamiliar even more unfamiliar, then the question is how should those that seek to resist this process respond? This is the central question of this book.

The first chapter 'September 11: Thoughts and Emotions' was written in the months following the terrorist attacks in New York and Washington DC. It was written as a response to the attacks themselves and the ensuing debate. Having written it, I recognized that there was some value in leaving it unedited as it provided a raw and honest first reflection as I attempted to come to terms with the attacks and the debate that followed.

The second chapter 'The Muslim Condition' is an essay on the central aspects of the challenges that Muslims in Britain face today and I seek to then provide an outline of a response that distinguishes between Muslim identity politics and Islamic humanism. I will contend in this book that it is Islamic humanism that may best help British Muslims navigate out of the perilous waters that we find ourselves in. The third chapter is a partly fictionalised account of my participation in an anti-war march in September 2002. This covers similar themes to the essay on 'The Muslim Condition' but provides a real life example of how such ideas can become practical.

The next two chapters are written as speeches. Chapter 4 is a speech that was given at the inaugural meeting of the Cambridge Muslim College on the ways in which the training of Islamic religious leaders needs to consider the variety of formative influences upon their congregations. Chapter 5 is an imagined speech given to the fictional Anglo-Liberal Fellowship of the South on the relationship between Islam and liberalism. Entitled 'Seven Faces of Freedom', it describes seven ways in which a Muslim can experience freedom.

The next three chapters focus on the issues of community cohesion, integration and multiculturalism. 'Muslims and the social' (Chapter 6) is a review essay on the recent academic debate on Muslims and multicultural policy. Chapter 7 is a speech at an event given by the author on the topic of considering the relevance of culture to public policy. Chapter 8 is a short fictional piece 'Finding a Saviour for a City in Need' about how a policymaker in a Northern city attempts to find a way forward for the city in the aftermath of rioting. The final chapter is an interview in which I reflect back over the presidency of George W. Bush, or what I have termed 'the Bush years'.

There are many people whom I should acknowledge as contributing towards the ideas in this book. I have benefited from the advice, conversations and writings of many people over the years. Sheikh Nuh Keller, Sheikh Abdal Hakim Murad and Sheikh Hamza Yusuf have all had a profound impact upon my understanding and practice of the religion. I am, like many others of my generation, deeply indebted to them. Professor Serge Moscovici, Professor Robert Farr and Professor Stuart Hall have helped to provide me with an intellectual architecture which will be familiar to anyone who knows their work. Their contributions to the sociology of knowledge have helped me immensely in attempting to make sense of my own situation. Professor Tariq Modood has also been helpful to me in his project to think through the ways in which liberal political theory could make room for a Muslim presence. I would like to acknowledge the kind permissions of the Cambridge Muslim College and of the *Muslim World Book Review* to reproduce in amended form the two respective publications: 'Some Reflections on Principles of Islamic Education within a Western Context', CMC Papers No.1, December 2008, for Chapter 4; and 'Muslims and the Social', *MWBR*, 28/4: 6-16, for Chapter 6. There are, of course, many more people to whom I am indebted but have not mentioned here.

S.M. Atif Imtiaz
Bradford
April 2010

1 September 11: Thoughts and Emotions[1]

In the confusion of wartime in which we are caught up, relying as we must on one-sided information, standing too close to the great changes that have already taken place or are beginning to, and without a glimmering of the future that is being shaped, we ourselves are at a loss as to the significance of the impressions which press in upon us and as to the value of the judgements which we form.[2]

Sigmund Freud

'The events of September 11.' 'What happened on September 11.' Such is the perceived enormity of that day that we cannot even categorise it; it remains beyond categorisation. The sheer violence of the initial impact followed by the heart-crushing collapse of the Twin Towers was more than this soul could bear, and I began to turn my face away as the TV editors repeatedly showed the images of death. For that's what they were, images of death, moments when hundreds if not thousands died.[3] I could not look on in awed fascination, as some have described.

Yet, I did feel some selfish concern at this moment. I thought: 'I hope some Muslims didn't do this, otherwise we're in trouble.' And so at the moment when thousands were dying, I was worrying about me. I am ashamed by my own selfishness and lack of humanity; and perhaps this leads on to my next question, for surely the events of September 11 did nothing more than throw up a thousand questions summed up in the words, 'What have we become?' Perhaps the saddest point to note in the aftermath is that instead of awakening everyone's heart to suffering, this event may have sent us further into our trenches from which we fire accusations at each other. It should have been a day when all self-critical souls looked into their own hearts and wondered whether they helped to bring this about. It should have been a day when suffering, by being brought right up to our faces, should have pulled humanity by the hand of humility from its present abyss.

> *O you who believe, stand up for justice, witnesses to Allah, even if it is against yourselves.*
>
> Qur'an, Surah An-Nisa, Verse 135

I felt guilty. I felt responsible, even though I have no connection to Osama bin Laden and the 'Jihad' group. The first time I ventured out after the attacks, I remember feeling more paranoid than normal. Looking intensely at others, with the thought that perhaps they were looking at me, holding me to account. I felt like approaching them and shaking them and shouting: 'But I don't agree with what was done! I was not involved!' And then, not for the first time in my life, and probably not for the last either, the way things are going, I realised what Durkheim meant when he said that collective representations are social and coercive.

I have lived through the Rushdie Affair when we were the vanguard of religious fascism. I have lived through the Gulf War when we were the fifth column. And perhaps most traumatically, I have lived through the war in Bosnia-Herzegovina, when we were passive onlookers to the murder of 200,000. I used to read newspapers, but stopped during the war in Bosnia-Herzegovina. I couldn't read anymore. Rape after rape. Murder after murder. I still vividly remember walking past the *Evening Standard* hoardings next to the news-stands at London tube stations before and after the fall of Srebrenica. I remember the day before it fell, the adverts announced: 'Srebrenica About to Fall!'

Similarly, on the day itself, 'Serb Troops Enter Srebrenica!' A few days later: 'Thousands of Men and Boys "Missing" in Srebrenica!' All the while, the commuters flowed back and forth, striding past the news, too busy, too tired and probably not deeply bothered.[4] Those days were maddening for me. As was the Gulf War, at the beginning of which George Bush had proclaimed: 'Our quarrel is not with the people of Iraq', which was before a million (half of them children) were killed through US-led sanctions. How I maintained my sanity, I don't know. In fact I remember on 10th September, thinking to myself, that bearing in mind the number of Muslims who have died in the last few decades (several million), Muslims generally have been very patient. But that was before the Towers fell. Perhaps what was so maddening for Muslims was the absence of argument and the lack of voice. I couldn't speak. If I did, no one listened. I was the wrong colour for a start, and I come from 'Paki'-land.

There is an underlying religious feeling to this conflict, even if it may ultimately not be about Christianity and Islam. The Twin Towers fell, and religious people believe that God permitted it to happen as He permits all human actions, good and bad, ours and theirs. The Taliban similarly withdrew from the cities and the Northern Alliance took over. God similarly permitted this to happen. The nervous post-hoc interpretation of both actions as either signifying God's pleasure or displeasure reminds me of Weber's analysis of the Protestant ethic, and how success in capitalist activity was the mark of God's pleasure in this life and success in the Next. It is as if the unfolding events are somehow indicative of who has the Truth, and whom it is that God is ultimately pleased with.

* * * * *

So why are we where we are today? I remember attending a conference in London in 1993 at which Ernest Gellner and François Burgat spoke.[5] Gellner said that the two main events of the twentieth century were the fall of Marxism and the rise of Islam. No doubt Islam has confounded key sociological thinkers such as Durkheim, Marx and Weber who argued that as secularisation as a function of modernity progresses, religion must go into decline. Islam's answer to that has been 'Count us out.' When I asked the sociologist Anthony Giddens in an interview why this was so, his reply was, 'Well the theorists were wrong about it, weren't they?' So religion is here to stay. The question then is: how to deal with it? More specifically, for those whose moral order is based upon liberalism: how to deal with political Islam? There is no doubt that there has been an awakening within Muslim countries in the last few decades, and Islamic movements have achieved varying degrees of success. The example that is closest to the point that I wish to make here is that of Algeria. After the FIS had walked through the first round of elections with a victory that would make Tony Blair jealous, the army stepped in and cancelled the elections. (Note a liberal paradox: the right of the individual Rushdie must be upheld, but the right of the nation Algeria can be ignored.) The apologetics of Western writers stated that Islam was simply anti-liberal, women were being oppressed, hands chopped off, and the rest. So even if the people wanted Islam, they must not be allowed to have it. And so democracy works to a lesser extent in most of the Muslim world with the aid of Western intelligence agencies. (Whence the disingenuous claim of Israel being the only democracy in the Middle East. First of all, democracy is not allowed in most of the Muslim world, thanks to the Western governments. Secondly, what is the point of being a democracy if one cannot treat other human beings with respect?) At the same conference, François Burgat spoke of bilateral radicalisation.[6] This is the idea that the moderates would attempt to work through the political process, be prevented by the respective governments' imaginative use of law (cf. Turkey and Egypt), so that sections of the movement would become radicalised and move outside the political process. This historically has lead to the formation of the Jihad movement of which Osama bin Laden is a charismatic leader. Calling for the overthrow of corrupt governments, the Jihad movement has grown over the last few years as injustice after injustice has been piled up in the Muslim world. (The second area of activity for the Jihad movement has been in Muslim minority situations such as Kashmir, Palestine and the Caucasus.) But effectively what has happened is that sections of political Islam have been radicalised towards extra-judicial violence, and the relative rise of the Jihad group has meant, in one sense, that oppression in Muslim lands has been successful. I am reminded of that game I used to play without much success in Blackpool. A two-penny piece had to be inserted through a slot at the top of a machine and the coin fell down onto or alongside a pile of coins. A machine moved the pile along as the coins hung on one side over a ledge. If my coin could move the pile along, five coins might fall. Maybe (and usually) not. The coins falling from the top of the machine are the numerous injustices heaped upon the Muslim world, and the coins that fall over the edge are the terrorists.

We have all been radicalised over the last decade or so, at least discursively. Who could not have been, after the Gulf War, Bosnia, Chechnya, Kashmir, and now Afghanistan, etcetera, etcetera. For how long can we bear the etceteras?[7] But – and this is where most media commentators miss the point – Islam is not a religion of violence. It teaches us to control our anger, to withhold it, to be patient through prayer. Because if Islam was a religion of violence and advocated insurrection, then I and many, many others would have become violent by now. Because the pain has been maddening. Five thousand children in Iraq every month. There have been times when I could not sleep because of this number. The disgust and shame that this number brought upon me has impelled me towards great anger. But I have controlled myself, as have the millions of practising, angry Muslim youth all over the world. Why? Because my religion has told me to control myself, and what my religion teaches me is sacred, full stop.

The play *Iranian Nights* written by Tariq Ali and Howard Brenton and performed in the aftermath of the Rushdie Affair suggested that the refugee turns to religion because he feels rejected:

Now I live in Notting Hill, with my mum. She is not well. The terror, the fear have broken her. Who can understand the fate of the prisoner and the poor who have fled from hate to a nowhere in the West, a nowhere in the rain? Who can understand our pain? Why does the West think it can do no wrong and expect the refugee to be superhumanly strong, more tolerant, more wise than any human being can be? It's a miracle that so many of us do have the strength to bear the abuse, bear the blind ignorance of what we are and where we come from. A miracle! That only a few have gone fanatic! That only a few rave about the satanic! Therefore, the more who speak out, the better. The more! The more! The better! About the profound matter of the nature of God and man, speak out as best you can! What finer sound is there than a human being singing against cruelty! Against hate![8]

It is not a miracle that we have not become terrorists; it is simpler than that. Islam prevents us from doing so.

The argument that has been proposed post-September 11 suggests that Islam is inherently violent, and that this is why these Muslims committed such acts of violence: they were acting on Islamic teachings. There is justification within Islam for these acts – that is the claim being made. If we are to play in an equal field, then does this mean that Christianity can justify the IMF or the sanctions against Iraq? Or Judaism justify Israel's militarism? Let's not let the secularists get away with this. Would the religion of the selfish gene justify sanctions against Iraq? The fact of the matter is that if there are one billion Muslims, at least a 100 million take Islam seriously, one in 10, and violence is not the norm in Muslim society. The twentieth century's violence was mainly European, not Islamic. We have not responded to the numerous events of the last decade with acts of violence. In fact our response has always been one of restraint, and, unbelievably, dialogue.

The issue of sleepers is an interesting one. I would suggest that instead of sleepers being conscious, recruited members of a secret network, we could do ourselves a favour by examining the social nature of this phenomenon. I would suggest that a total climate of oppression has led to a situation in which there are millions of sleepers all over the planet. They are not members of al-Qaida. They are ordinary practising Muslims. They become activated once they cannot take it anymore and they lose touch with the Sacred Law. The American government is chasing a mirage if it thinks that al-Qaida is as organised as it suggests. This is the real problem for the American government: how to deal with a massive social phenomenon. (To be anti-hegemony is not in itself a bad thing; Foucault felt able to applaud Khomeini for being anti-hegemony.) If I were an anthropologist wandering around Washington at the moment, I would suggest that the bureaucrats of government agencies such as the State Department, the FBI and the CIA have a fetish for organisation. They need to construct the mirage of an organised body so that they can investigate it.

* * * * *

'Are you with the civilised world or with the naan-civilised world?' These words of James Rubin, the former US Assistant Secretary of State, still ring clear in my mind. He said these words, echoing Ehud Barak's, across the discussion floor on the day of the attack. (How strange that Barak happened to be in the BBC offices at the time of the attack, as was reported. What was he doing there: congratulating the BBC for its objective coverage of the Middle East? And how strange, that Colin Powell echoed the same words in interviews following the attack. This was spin too well spun.) So suddenly civilisation was on the agenda. 'Are you civilised or uncivilised?' Why the resurrection of pre-colonial justificatory discourse?[9] What irritated me most about Rubin was that this was the same man who was paid to justify the sanctions against Iraq. This is civilisation. The hijacking of language to cover mass murder. Call me uncivilised.

Well, I can't let this discussion on civilisation pass without mentioning Lord Douglas Hurd, former Secretary of State for the Home Office and later on the Foreign and Commonwealth Office. During the Rushdie Affair, he said to Muslims gathered at Birmingham Central Mosque:

You clearly feel as if the most sacred things of your faith have been insulted and wounded. You feel shocked and you feel angry. But to turn such protests towards violence as has been suggested, not, I agree, in this country but elsewhere, or the threat of violence, I must say, is wholly unacceptable. Talks of death, talks of arrows being directed at hearts, such talk is vicious, it's repugnant to civilised men or women.[10]

It was Douglas Hurd who was influential as one of the politicians who argued that the Bosnian Muslims must be refused the right to arm themselves. That would lead to an escalation in the war, he argued (his term was 'a level killing field'). Meanwhile, many died. Imagine my feelings when I read Francis Wheen's article which related how the same Hurd had become deputy chairman of the NatWest Markets which early in 1996 'concluded a deal with Milosevic to privatise Serbia's post and telecommunication system and manage the country's national debt. NatWest's fee was said to be in the region of $10 million'.[11] Call me uncivilised.

* * * * *

Terrorism. Global political structures use words like 'terrorism' so much that their semantic utility tends to decline sharply. The popular definition is 'the use of violence by madmen to secure anti-democratic ends'. Of course, terrorism is directly and inversely related to democracy, at least rhetorically. Hence the frequent sloganeering about 'democracy and freedom'. (A friend of mine said recently that he gets worried whenever they start talking about democracy and freedom, because it means that they are about to bomb a Third World country. He was right.) The terrorists are against democracy and freedom. Our right to be free. Superficially, this may ring true. But how about changing 'free' to 'rich'? 'These terrorists hate our freedom (wealth)! They don't want us to be free (rich). We must fight those who are willing to attack us just because we want to be free (rich)'. Make any more sense?

Those persons who talk most about human freedom are those who are actually most blindly subject to social determination, inasmuch as they do not in most cases suspect the profound degree to which their conduct is determined by their interests.[12]

* * * * *

'The horror. The horror.' Colonel Kurtz's last words. I wonder sometimes about their meaning. Is this the horror of the civilised man grown savage, or the horror of the corrupting influence of power? Or both? As we journey through the labyrinth of political error that has led us to where we are, the question to be asked is: is the horror on our side or theirs? The answer, of course, is that the horror is on their side. Have we become savage in the pursuit of civilisation? Has power corrupted us in our pursuit of egalitarianism? The practical answer to this question lies in the machination of modernity. I would suggest that just as knowledge and power are two sides of the same coin according to Michel Foucault, in the same way, violence and distance are also two sides of the same coin in the discussion on terrorism and modernity. The terrorist terrorises us because he bridges this gap in the late modern era, whereas the objective of modernity is to make the equation of violence over distance tend as much towards zero as possible. The violent act committed by the state has to be out of sight, out of mind and out of discourse (hence the present discussions about press access to casualties in Afghanistan, and the resentment against Al Jazeera). The sanctions against Iraq work so well because the distance between the act of violence and the actor is so great that the thread linking the two is too tenuous for the frail democratic sense. The 'terrorist' act decreases this distance almost to zero. Suffering, of course, does not look to the name of the sender. But for some strange reason, we are today living in times when the 'terrorist' form of violence exacts more horror. The drama of the moment holds our attention.

Here the word 'terrorism' requires some comment. It is a word that, like its twin 'fundamentalist', doesn't really mean

9

much. Ask someone what they mean when they use the word and present different scenarios to question their definition and you'll get the picture. 'Terrorism' according to the lay definition means 'the use of violence by madmen to secure anti-democratic ends'. I use the term 'madmen' specifically. The suggestion according to this essentially right-wing definition is that 'terrorists' are those people who are responsible for their actions because they have decided through rationalisation to commit acts of violence. The simultaneous description of them as 'madmen' confounds their ambivalent reception, for 'madness' limits the agency of the individual and renders them free of law. Perversely, madness can be a route to freedom. A more left-wing definition of 'terrorism' would be 'politics by desperate means' – the desperate under total political and military oppression resort to acts of individual and extreme violence. Blair has entered this debate (and hence tacitly admitted the problem of defining terrorism) by offering the following definition in his answer to a question about the war in Afghanistan at Prime Minister's *Question Time* (7th November 2001): 'Terrorism maximises loss of civilian life, we minimise loss of civilian life.' Netanyahu had offered the same definition on BBC2's *Newsnight* a week earlier (31st October 2001).

The use of the word 'terrorism' by subaltern agents is a valiant attempt to re-focus concern towards universal suffering but the word has meaning only in reference to the powerful. There's a word that we don't hear much of. Power. Why? An open discussion on the nature of the relationship of terrorism to power would of course lead to the subaltern victory. Hence, the absence of discussion. For 'terrorism' is the violence of the powerless, while 'militarism' is the violence of the powerful. And since anything that can establish a relation to the nation-state can automatically assume authority, 'militarism' reflects the order of things, while 'terrorism' reflects disorder. The *Oxford English Dictionary* defines 'terrorism' as 'the use of violence and intimidation for political purposes'. Interestingly, this definition does not introduce the question of the level of violence.

Recent reports suggest that the American intelligence agencies are reconsidering the use of torture as a tool to extract information. Simultaneously, the newly-introduced human rights act in Britain is being set aside so that suspects can be imprisoned forever without trial. Well, this at least confirms to Muslims (for whom this act is primarily intended) what they have always thought, that they are insufficiently human to warrant human rights. Both are examples of extreme policies that are practised in the Middle East on a regular basis. It seems that the policies have come home. Is this reverse globalisation or the boomerang effect?

* * * * *

Gustav Ichheiser has written about the difference between ideology in principle and ideology in practice in American culture.[13] Ideology in principle is democracy; ideology in practice is nationalism.[14] These past few months have thrown up this distinction to a remarkably clear degree. The talk has been of democracy, but the symbolism has been that of nationalism. The American flag is outselling the Afghani flag. And it is this distinction between rhetoric and practice that allows the bombing to begin and continue. 'You killed American citizens, we must kill you.' This base nationalist feeling is perhaps the most dangerous idea roaming the planet and it is this same feeling that punctures any attempt to achieve humanitarian sensitivity. Ultimately, history and geography decide who can be a human being in practice. In rhetoric, we are all human beings, as human rights discourse usurps the old-fashioned democracy slogans; but, in practice, human beings are unequal. There are currency rates for human lives. And I think recent events have shaken these markets. So exactly how many Afghans are equal to one American?

'Not one American or British soldier has been killed so far,' crow the hawks. If the Americans had sent their soldiers into battle, it might have been a different story. Instead, they used the Northern Alliance to fight the Taliban, Afghan against Afghan, because Americans are worth more. We do value certain lives more than others, and this is because of the way that we interpret individualism. The ideology of human rights being derivative of Kantian rationalism assumes individuals are mutually replaceable, all equal in front of the UN. But, in reality, human psychology does not work like this. We may say that all humans are equal, but, in reality, humans are different, and it is culture that determines the ascription of value. Culture strikes through human rights discourse. That is why the deaths of New Yorkers mean more so much more to viewers than the deaths of Afghani villagers or Iraqi children. (Those alert to media imagery will have noticed that after the angry, shouting crowd of Muslim youth and the wailing, pleading *hijabis*, has come a third image, that of children training for warfare, the implicit question following on from Israeli spin being 'What kind of people train children to kill?', thus implicitly justifying the murder of Muslim children.) But New York is the home to global culture. *Friends* and *Sex and the City* both have a New York-style backdrop to their narratives of life. Superman, Spiderman and Batman were all New Yorkers. We share, or aspire to, that culture. We can relate to them because they invade our TV screens regularly. We live and make sense of our lives through their stories. And now we feel their suffering, because we can relate to them. More, certainly, than we can relate to a Third-Worlder. It is this social psychological reality that punctures the ascending balloon of human rights discourse. Culture brings people together, and forces people apart. (Kant is important as an ancestor because he has been described as the founder of the modern concept of race.)[15]

Compare what the Catholics in Northern Ireland, the Palestinians, the Kashmiris and the Chechens have received and one begins to realise that there are decreasing levels of justice in this world. I suggest that 'justice' (minus the infinite) needs to be heard of a bit more. This word doesn't really match well with human rights discourse, mainly because human rights discourse is so frequently useful in serving hegemonic powers. Human rights activists say that you can have economic or political justice only if you agree with our way of doing things, that is to say, you can't have your cake, even if you want to eat it.[16] An attempt to universalise human rights discourse is essentially an attempt to globalise the Enlightenment project, especially in the notion that there are only rights for individuals, and this is highly problematic.

For those who wish to discuss the real nature of things, a knowledge of economics is necessary. Oil money, the WTO, the IMF, the numerous trade agreements, and the rapid liberalisation of Third World markets at the expense of local business: who is the thief? One doesn't have to be a Marxist to recognise that economic globalisation is proceeding in an unbalanced manner. The ideology in practice means that the South Carolina farmer is rich because the African or the Indian farmer is poor. For those who remain unconvinced, I direct them to the writings of Susan George and Vandana Shiva.[17] The US's approach to globalisation has simultaneously included the retreat from the Kyoto Protocol on the cutting of greenhouse gas emissions, the retreat from the anti-biological warfare treaty, the retreat from the anti-racism conference and the retreat from the anti-ballistic weapons treaty. So the US is interested in economic globalisation, but not, it seems, in other forms. John Locke wrote: 'In the beginning, all the world was America'[18] (referring, ironically, to the then relatively insignificant accumulation of wealth); today perhaps it would be: 'The whole world is becoming America', and tomorrow, 'America is the world'. This does not mean that the US is unified on these matters. It is just that big business decides things in Washington. It is the study of the interaction between democracy and economics that I wish to encourage here; but what should we call it? How about demonomics?

You may accuse me here of being anti-American. I would be disappointed. Much of what I wish to say about America is already an intrinsic part of American discourse, whether it is in relation to anti-globalisation, democracy, war or Muslims. Bobby Sayyid points out in his book: 'There is a convergence between 'internal' critics of the West and the Islamist critique of Western hegemony.'[19] This is an internal dispute whose ramifications are played out amongst innocents living in other parts of the world. This leads on to two interconnected points.

First of all, the idea of the US being isolationist. So what exactly does the CIA do? How can true democrats tolerate the existence of an organisation whose central purpose is interference in the affairs of other countries? How many CIA agents are currently aiding the numerous Muslim governments against their own populations (e.g. in Turkey, Egypt, Pakistan, Indonesia)? Why do no political observers and analysts talk about the influence of the intelligence services? It is of course politically impolite to ask such questions, but I only do so for the interests of the political rights of other countries.

The second issue is of the nature of politics in the US and the UK. One of the more depressing sights over the last few weeks has been the closing of political ranks. Perhaps there are no greater political issues in our times. However the three main British political parties have virtually fallen over each other in agreement post-September 11. The same is true for America. In 2000, the world witnessed an intense polarisation in the political sphere as Democrats and Republicans bickered about the Florida recount. But today they are united in the 'war against terror'. Anthony Giddens' notion of political debate in the late modern era as being beyond left and right proved true for much of the 1997–2001 parliament.[20] Tony Blair's Labour Party managed to occupy the centre ground. The Tories, in their perplexity, shifted to the right. The debates on key issues such as public services became a real bore. Arguing over fine details and intricate numbers, both Tony Blair and William Hague defied the common man in debate after debate to understand what exactly it was that they were disagreeing about.

But recent years have witnessed the emergence of a new political space, one outside the normal consensus. This is represented by the anti-globalisation movement. It takes seriously the effects of one nation upon the rest of the world, and it calls on citizens of one particular country to audit their effect, primarily economic, on other human beings, which means that it takes the language of human rights seriously, and it disregards in one clean sweep the nationalist agenda. One cannot help but think, while listening to the political rhetoric coming out of

Washington and London, that we are hearing the last cries of nationalism before we approach the post-nationalist era. I think this political space has arrived and needs to be articulated and expanded. The Blair government is attempting to carve out a new political space for itself and in doing so it wishes to afford some kind of morality, an ideology in principle. But there are at least two obstacles. Firstly, 'ethical foreign policy' was one attempt at this, but once the government discovered the price of human rights, little more was heard of the phrase. Secondly, the government has released information on policy shifts with regard to nuclear processing, Railtrack, tuition fees and asylum vouchers in the immediate aftermath of the attacks, highlighting the interaction between policy and manipulation. The government, it seems, does not have the necessary moral courage, though it has a huge democratic mandate. If within the modern democratic framework a strong government cannot afford morality, then who can?

* * * * *

A noticeable characteristic on the part of Jim Liberal is the refusal to engage with detail, especially in relation to international issues. A friend of mine was once talking to a non-Muslim friend of his who was slightly upset with Muslims. After my friend managed to give his side of the story, the non-Muslim's response was 'We should blow the whole world up and start again.' The refusal to deal with detail as in the case of much Middle Eastern politics may be a source of much humour for people like me, but ultimately, it remains as a tragic wall that bars political progress. 'Both sides are at fault.' 'Two wrongs don't make a right.' As if all wrongs are equivalent.

This myopic interpretation is common in international debate. But closer examination reveals that such platitudes are irrelevant at best. For example, let us take two forms of violence and murder. The attacks on the World Trade Centre and the Pentagon, and the sanctions against Iraq. Both required planning and execution. An attention to detail is necessary.

15

But here the similarities end. One act of violence ended in a moment. The other has lasted for 10 years. One act of violence has the backing of a government which is democratically elected. The other has the backing of a small network. And this is where the strange nature of social attribution reveals itself. Governments representing nations (i.e. the majority) are not accountable according to the press, but Muslims and Islam are accountable for the actions of a small religious minority (even though the media is doing much to counterbalance this effect). So responsibility is differentially distributed. Strange, but true. In fact, the Archbishop of Canterbury, representing the majority of British Christians, supported the bombing of Afghanistan, whereas violence has only ever been advocated by minority Muslim spokesmen. Perhaps stereotyping is only against the weak, that is, it lies in the hands of the powerful and the majoritarian, the hegemonic? Of course, one could be cynical, and read political actors through the reverse of their professed statements. So Tony Blair appeals to the middle classes although he is the leader of the Labour party. Similarly, John Major celebrated his Brixton beginnings, though he was Conservative Prime Minister. So what does this say about Tony Blair's religion and the current government? (Note how Blair began by using the anti-drugs argument as a pretext for war in Afghanistan, later permitting his Home Secretary to decriminalise cannabis.)

The argument regarding the Holocaust as a supreme evil because it employed the machinations of modernity towards suffering is, I believe, a strong one; although I do have a problem with the implicit valorisation of rationality, as if it could, if left alone, never lead to evil. The sanctions against Iraq have killed at least one million – that's a sixth of the Holocaust – and I think that as such the sanctions qualify to join the Evil Hall of Fame. The machinations of modernity have been used here as well, including the proper functioning of democracy. How many times have the sanctions been raised in the Commons, and how many times have MPs ignored them while eyeing front bench positions? Democracy can walk shoulder to shoulder with mass murder if the thinking masses and the chattering classes are drunk on the wine of banality.

* * * * *

There is a problem with commenting on recent events, and it is to do with the interaction between media studies and international relations. The Glasgow University Media Group has conducted some research on the reporting of war, but to my knowledge (and I would love to know of instances that prove otherwise) there has been no major piece of work on the relation between information dissemination and time after a major event. One opportunity is provided by the recent publication of a book on the conflict in Bosnia by Brendan Simms, a Cambridge historian, examining the nature of political decision-making that permitted so much mayhem.[21] One could compare the content and style of discourse within this book with the newspaper coverage at the time, and see what differences, if any, emerge. Similarly one could compare a recent article detailing US political decision-making in relation to Rwanda with US newspaper coverage of the genocide at the time.[22]

We all know that the first casualty of war is truth. However what I am wishing to suggest here is that the type of discourse changes dramatically as one moves further and further away from the source event as truth begins to appear without disguise. Secret files are released, ex-ministers are more open, shocked bureaucrats leak sensitive information, international friendships fall apart. And the truth begins to appear. The huge wave of news information post-September 11 is enough to drown one under detail after detail. However, for those who are interested in the real nature of things, the best thing to do is to stand back, treat media speculation for what it is, and to buy a few books on the history of politics in the Middle East and American foreign policy.

* * * * *

I remember once having a discussion with one of my teachers about the nature of reality in our times. He was working on the social psychology of globalisation and implicit to his work is the principle that the picture of the Earth from the moon is enough to convince people that the Earth is round. (Like millions of others I have received the e-mail which tries to convince me that NASA faked it, but let's leave that issue aside – I am not a flat-earther.) I remember discussing the efficacy of imagery as proof with him. I was suggesting that as computer imaging develops, it will become more difficult to distinguish between true and false images. The Gulf War made this issue real and perhaps this is what Baudrillard meant by his essay *The Gulf War Did Not Take Place*: he was satirising the postmodern contempt for suffering.[23] Of course, the events of September 11 have turned this issue on its head. Many people will have seen the films that can be related symbolically to the planes crashing into the twin towers. 'The Towering Inferno' has a burning building about to collapse. 'Independence Day' has scenes in which buildings representing American nationalism are blown up. 'The Siege' has a secret enemy cell plotting to kill innocent civilians in New York. 'Executive Decision' has Muslim terrorists hijacking a plane.

On September 11, all the story lines merged into one in a single dramatic moment. 'It was just like a movie!' This was heard often in the aftermath of the attacks. The reality wasn't: it was worse, much worse, because not only did the hijackers manage to combine the worst aspects of each film narrative, but they also managed to kill thousands. That doesn't happen in the movies. And now films are being shelved because the weak distinction between fact and fiction isn't standing up under so much scrutiny. There is something of the self-fulfilling prophecy about this. For years, Muslims have complained of negative representation. There were no major terrorist acts. Now, of course, some people will say, 'You see, we were right!' But they are wrong. Gordon Allport has written of the self-fulfilling nature of representation (though it may be mediated by ambivalence) and it seems that this repeated representation of Muslims as terrorists has become a reality.[24] The distinction between representation and reality has been further blurred by references to Bin Laden's similarity to Blofeld, the arch-enemy of James Bond.[25] Even a Downing Street source said after the Northern Alliance went into Kabul: 'Things are going to be a bit messy. This was never going to unfold like a Steven Spielberg movie.'[26]

One obvious winner in the past months has been the media. No doubt much will be written in the years to come about the media and September 11. There are many areas for analysis: the overlap between fact and fiction, the effects of the repetitive display of images of extreme violence, the symbolism of the attack, the representation of otherness, the challenge of language, and the totalisation of discourse. Of these, it is the latter that most interests me. This was probably the first time since the globalisation of the media and the arrival of the internet and satellite TV that discourse was total. Meaning that there was no space for difference. Poor Pakistan! The whole world was staring at Pakistan with accusative eyes on the Thursday after the Tuesday. 'Either you are with us or against us!' And who could disagree in the face of such total carnage, the destruction of two buildings that championed America like no other? Or was it the number of lives that were lost that constituted the real disaster? I can't help feeling that the destruction of the two buildings means more to some than the three thousand lives. How could there be disagreement after such total mayhem? And total mayhem means total discourse. We could only think through the words and the images that we were seeing.

The media, which usually struggles to capture major audiences, suddenly found itself serving captive audiences. There was no other topic of conversation (whence the British government's timed press releases). The language devoured us all. Muslims were objectified as a global Other at that moment, through the image of Osama bin Laden. Muslims generally have no problem opposing hegemony, in fact we quite enjoy it, yet the horror did not escape us. We felt the horror too. But the bombings on Afghanistan (which were presumably ordered to meet public opinion before the month ran out) changed the moral landscape again and the total language no longer exerted its hold over us. I think that Western governments lost the one opportunity they had to make serious headway towards conflict resolution.

* * * * *

The acceptance of Islam can only come about after Western agencies cease to caricaturise Islam and the Sharia. (See Roxanne Euben for a grown-up discussion of comparative political theory in which she examines the similarities between Islamist political discourse and the writings of Arendt, Bell, Bellah and Taylor.[27]) Cultural theorists would say that I am being too optimistic. The increase in stereotyping and caricaturing is related to the increasing threat of a certain sort of 'political Islam'. That is, as this Islam advances on to the public scene, stereotypes will be constructed in order to make it seem threatening, different, as alter to our ego. The Taliban were used precisely for this reason. Story after story hit the papers emphasising their complete otherness to an idyllic, middle-class, Surrey lifestyle. How representative were the Taliban of the world's one billion Muslims? Or the numerous expressions of political Islam? And how representative were the media stories about the Taliban of the Taliban themselves? I'll return to this later. I remember a series on BBC2 in 2000 called 'Behind the Lines' in which Sean Langan, a journalist, visited Afghanistan, Iran, Iraq and Palestine, interviewing a series of Others. The argument being put forward was that here is a line which divides us from a fascistic Them (in almost every programme Langan spoke about how he could not say what he wanted, or about how he was being followed, Orwellian style), and hence we have two blocs. The democratic, secular West and the fascist Islamic East. Of course, had he visited Turkey, Egypt, Tunisia, Algeria and the like, the argument about political freedom and Islam would have been turned on its head. The line is not so clear anymore, the convenient story not so believable. He did, as it happens, visit Egypt, but according to inside sources the BBC pulled the programme for 'technical reasons'. I am no great defender of political Islam: the Islamist cake will most probably be a modernist cake in postmodernist times (with an Islamic cherry on top), but surely other nations have rights to representative government?[28] The Western media's support for what in many cases are appallingly tyrannical regimes belies their commitment to freedom.

But this is not the end of it. The above position is justified by suggesting that Muslims are actually against freedom, and especially the freedom of women. This is another area requiring grown-up discussion. Feminists who rage against the Muslim treatment of women monopolise the banner of freedom (so that the girl who wears hijab is oppressed but the girl who wears a miniskirt is free) while concurrently failing to recognise the involvement of women in the Muslim resurgence. Instead, desperate lists are produced and fake scenarios rehearsed detailing oppression after oppression. The arguments that such feminists propose assume an individualism that is crude and rooted deeply in Protestant culture valuing the public role and work ethic of the self-sufficient male. And all must converge on this model. The grown-up discussion on individualism versus communitarianism and gender relations allows for a bit more flexibility. Crude individualisms advanced as Enlightenment-inspired positivist truths are not the answer. Two questions to be asked here are: is it necessary for one discourse which is culturally specific to one society and historical experience to be universalised? The feminists would surely reply by pointing out that this is exactly what religion assumes. So feminism (a crude version) is now a religion? Secondly: can feminists be racists as well? Well, the feminist community has been there before and the answer is yes. Feminism does inform the present debate and it seems that it legitimises the bombing, such that, 'Because the Taliban oppress their women, we can bomb them.' Is it any wonder that the papers took issue with the BBC's *Question Time* immediately after September 11 by printing a large picture of the sister in hijab who spoke assertively against American foreign policy? What could they not tolerate: her opinion or her challenge to their stereotype of Muslim women?

> And blessed are they who in the main
> This faith, even now, do entertain.
> Wordsworth, 'Ode to Duty'

A fairer representation of an assertive Islam is a huge problem, and I am not sure that enough in the West have a sufficient sense of fair play for this to happen. So perhaps there is another way. Let us recognise that we do accept the Sharia when money (or oil) is involved as in the case of Saudi Arabia, and so it is possible when it suits our interests. Perhaps, I am simplifying the matter. An ideological analysis would suggest that the two master signifiers in the Muslim world are Israel and oil. The value of any country and its applicant leader depends on their answers to these two questions. So a Muslim leader can be good if he accepts the Oslo peace process, even if he is bad for his own population. A Muslim leader can similarly be good if he is co-operative towards our oil needs, even if he is corrupt. The Muslim masses know this, and they know that they are on the receiving end of both policies. The caricaturing of Islamic law is merely one of several ideological strategies aimed at maintaining the position of the master signifiers. The right of any Muslim country to self-determination is easily brushed aside. Recent events show that attempts to maintain this hegemony have lead to increasing radicalisation and therefore more violence. I would suggest that an accommodation with political Islam in fact serves the long-term interests of Western stability. Otherwise, radicalisation and the cycle of violence will continue.

Cycle of violence. Now there's an interesting phrase, used repeatedly by the US State Department over the last year in regard to the conflict between the Israelis and the Palestinians. 'We urge both sides to show restraint.' 'We call on both sides to cease this cycle of violence.' No right, no wrong. No strong, no weak. Only a 'cycle of violence.' There has been a cycle of violence in the Middle East for the past three decades. The US and other Western governments built up Saddam Hussein and his army in order to fight Iran in the eighties, and then spent the nineties bombing them down again. They simultaneously trained Osama bin Laden and friends, and are now currently bombing them.[29] Who will we train now in order to bomb them in 2012? The American foreign policy wonks are probably repeating the Hardy line to each other: 'That's another fine mess you got me into!' Which way to turn? So much danger around. If I was scared of nature, I would use the analogy of dropping someone in the middle of the Amazon jungle and asking them to make their way to the sea.

* * * * *

'Give me your hand!'
'I can't!'
'If we live, we live together; if we die, we die together!'
'I'm scared.'
'Scared of what?'
'Of you.'
'You don't know me.'
'I know about you.'
'Give me your hand!'

It has been open season against Islam. Writers who normally struggle to put a few hundred words together and labour to find an issue of sufficient importance, have been presented with an opportunity to provide their analysis of a world event. Except that most of them don't have a clue. Especially in relation to the issue that supposedly lies at the heart of this crisis: Islam and the West. Assumptions, stereotypes, even ignorance become acceptable replacements for informed opinion. For example, Peter Beaumont writes of Bin Laden sharing Khomeini's conception of Islamic revolution (e.g. the role of the jurist as a political leader) when most people who know a thing or two about both the Iranian revolution and the Jihad movement know that they don't agree at all. Salafism and Shi'ism have different notions of authority. But the trajectory of radicalism is too good a narrative to ignore, as Khomeini passes the baton relay-style to Bin Laden. (Interestingly Rashid Rida becomes a co-radical in the same article!)[30] Similarly, Salman Rushdie, that great expert on Islam, wrote like a Tory proselyte, erupting with right-wing discourse all the way through his article.[31] Not that I am a leftie. But correct me if I am wrong – wasn't Rushdie a leftie in a previous decade? Note, then, the shift to the right-wing talk of 'Let's smoke 'em out!' It seems that the terrorists are not the only desperate people. Well, one interesting point to note from Rushdie's essay is his list that proves that 'fundamentalists' (*sic*) are tyrants. Leaving aside the confusing terminology (since it is the norm), he suggests in this list that Muslims are against accountable government. He is obviously ignorant of the Islamist claims of non-accountability against the Saudi and the Egyptian regimes. In fact, accountability is one of the most recurrent arguments of Islamists. (Other members of the list included beardlessness and sex. I can reassure Mr Rushdie that we are innocent on both accounts. On the first, women don't have to wear beards, and on the second, the Prophet encouraged sex as a religious act.) One should take note of how Rushdie's writing supports the hegemonic rationale for numerous corrupt Muslim governments. Thirdly, Henry Porter argues for the Eurocentric view (great timing!) that Islam needs to experience a reformation.[32] If he knew more about Islam then he would know that the closest thing that Islam has had to a reformation has led to the problems that he is trying to explain. But he doesn't.

The *Observer* and the *Guardian* would no doubt be upset. Why don't I criticise the real ignoramuses of other papers for their jingoistic, half-baked diatribes?[33] Exactly. I think I can get a conversation with the *Observer* and the *Guardian*, and their coverage on the whole has to be commended as brave and important. The secularists, much to my non-surprise, have managed to use these events to play their favourite game, 'Who can bash religion the most?' Of course, Richard Dawkins, Professor for the Public Understanding of Science (irony of ironies) at Oxford, always wins hands down. Religion, Mr Dawkins, is keeping the peace at the moment. The day we all follow his selfish gene hypothesis, much in the style of American foreign policy, will be the day that this world lurches much closer towards anarchy. But Mr Dawkins has not been alone. There have been numerous Muslim-bashers out roaming the pages, and I play a game with myself while reading their pieces. Two questions are to be asked of each: 'How many Muslim friends have they got?' and 'How many books on Islam have they read?' Of course, two ducks makes them expertly qualified. It is more amusing on TV: watching them mispronounce names, get their history wrong, their facts wrong, and stumble over the geography, but hey, here come the experts. If it wasn't so serious, but it is serious. Two-and-a-half cheers for Fred Halliday (no Islamophile) for at least being an expert.

Thinking about the recent Islam Week on BBC2, I remember the extent to which Islam and being Muslim oversignifies all other categories. Islam is a total discourse.[34] All actions have to be related back to God, and hence the futile attempt to philosophically (as opposed to politically, which is less of a problem) marry Islam with freedom, since ultimately all actions have to become subservient to God, if not now, then on the Day of Judgement. The human imperative is to reconcile free will with the Will of God. So for a Muslim, Islam is totalising, and if you ask me of the phenomenology of it, in a liberating sort of way. Yet, what is strange about the non-Muslim observation of Muslims is the extent to which Islam is so significant as the key source of categorisation. 'Do you do that because of your religion?' How often are we asked this? How often are we explained away because of some crude caricature of our faith? And how little are we actually heard? As national conversation on the television or in the newspapers seeks access into the phenomenology of so much that represents the alternative, there remains still an absence: 'What are Muslims like?'

Muslims may wonder what non-Muslims think about them. Zadie Smith's *White Teeth* provides an answer, albeit fictional. Joyce, a woolly middle-class do-gooder, decides to take in Millat, an angry, confused, young Muslim, for tutoring. She comes to the conclusion through the aid of her doctor friend Marjorie that Millat suffers from Attention Deficit Disorder: ADD. Joyce and Irie, a friend of Millat's, discuss how best to deal with him:

> 'Because if Marjorie's right, and it is ADD, he really needs to get to a doctor and some methylphenidate. It's a very debilitative condition'.
> 'Joyce, he hasn't got a disorder, he's just a Muslim. There are one billion of them. They can't all have ADD'.
> Joyce took a little gasp of air. 'I think you're being very cruel. That's exactly the kind of comment that isn't helpful'.[35]

I don't think that British or Western people are ignorant of Islam. It is not that they don't know, it is mostly that what they know is factually incorrect or unrepresentative.[36] They know, for example, about the fatwa, the book burning in Bradford, hands being chopped off, the stoning of adulterers and forced marriages. (They also know about the Alhambra, the Taj Mahal, *zakat* and Hajj but the scales are tipped heavily on one side.) There is enough mistrust of Islam for accusations to stick without checking, as Islam occupies the position of the feared, threatening, mistrusted Other. Edward Said provides some of the reasons for why this is the case.[37] These examples occupy the foreground of the Western imagination as it interacts with Muslims, such that as soon as a Muslim opens his mouth, the retort comes back: 'But what about the fatwa?' Trapped is he who doesn't have his answers already prepared. What is the point of dialogue beyond such retorts? Excusing, explaining, and apologising: 'But you don't understand ....'

Voltaire and Montesquieu differed in their understandings of the Ottoman Empire. For Montesquieu, the Ottoman Empire represented a phantasmic, despotic Other whereas Voltaire was more cautious.

> There is plainly no question here of splitting Voltaire and Montesquieu. On the level of evidence, Voltaire is right, and

without doubt the analysis of the Asiatic regimes developed by Montesquieu – be it the Ottoman, Persian, Mogul or Chinese empires – rests on partial information and partial interpretation. Correct though these criticisms may be, however, it seems to us none the less that they in no way detract from the force of the concept of despotism as elaborated and deployed by Montesquieu.[38]

There was a force to the false narrative which, it seems, is being replicated today. We live in a society in which visual culture dominates oral culture. As Gustav Ichheiser has observed: 'Looking at each other is the most primary form of conversation.'[39] Our eyes have taken over from our ears. The distance that separates us can be maintained by looking but not by hearing. Much of what we find out about others is through reading. It's so much easier than listening to someone, especially someone we might know. People don't talk to each other: they find out about each other through newspapers and books, and so misinformation is crucial in maintaining separation. I remember sitting across from a lady on a train in London. She was reading *White Teeth*. She might have been reading about Millat Iqbal, the young lad who gets wrapped up in a fundamentalist group called KEVIN (were they too illiterate to realise?), and through Smith's novel maybe she could have begun to understand why young Muslims become radicalised, like the young Muslim sitting opposite her? I doubt it. If modern cultures allowed for more open conversation, then maybe people would talk to each other on trains, even across differences. Who knows, we might even begin to understand each other a bit more.

Is there a fear of the Muslim voice? I remember watching *Question Time* after the attacks. I noticed the trepidation before a Muslim spoke. 'What will they say this time?' 'Will they be reasonable?' The silence before the storm. Except that usually there wasn't a storm. He or she would generally sound quite reasonable. But I remember the fear, I felt it myself, 'I hope they don't say anything stupid.' There is a fear of the Muslim voice, perhaps we are scared to hear criticism, perhaps we are afraid of their anger, perhaps they don't make sense. One point, though, to note about Osama bin Laden is that that old dictum has been proved true: 'If you say something often enough, people will learn how to pronounce it.'

The release of *Crouching Tiger, Hidden Dragon* in 2000 was met with public acclaim. The critics were pleased that a non-English language film had done so well. A film that was at ease in another culture was celebrated as marking the beginnings of Western openness (even though it was essentially replicating postmodern or Western narratives of gender). But just as the huge wooden doors of tolerance were being pushed open, along came the Taliban. The Taliban, of course, don't employ spin doctors. But this doesn't mean that media personnel don't make money from them. The Taliban have the unfortunate accolade of being the indirect employers of reverse-spin doctors. These are those who spin the message away from the desired result, and there's plenty of them. Their spinning has justified Western prejudices against other-worlders, and huge gates of tolerance have been shut again for another few years. The repetitive showing of images of violence and the easy stereotyping of 'bearded fanatics' and 'oppressed Muslim women' has reassured liberals that they are in fact right. This is not the only moral Other. One section of the liberal-left adopted the Taliban as their supreme moral Other. Another section has opted for the US as their supreme moral Other. Superficially, these two groups may seem similar except that their intended targets are poles apart. But I think further analysis will find that though both groups aim to occupy the same political space, their analyses are in fact diametrically opposed in terms of basic concepts, the most crucial being power.

The presence of Muslims in Britain has been raised again as questions are asked about our loyalty to the Queen. I look at this issue from a slightly different perspective. Imagine, in an ideal liberal world, there would be no Muslims in Britain. Instead, they would all live far away in distant countries which we could visit if we wanted to. We would not have to hear their constant complaining about rights, local and international; we would only have to endure their company at global conferences which only last for a few days. Things would be so much easier. I disagree. The most important contribution that the Muslim community makes to this country at present is not cultural (meaning the restaurants – why is it that multicultural events are always about pakoras and bhangra?) but political, though it should be spiritual. Our strong-mindedness may be irritating, but it serves to hold up the political parties, lobbies and commentators to their claims. We constantly remind politicians of the universal applicability of their pious hopes. We refuse to let easy answers slip away, we inform the debate with knowledge and experience, we place Britain (as a country that is still struggling with these debates) at the centre of the world discussion on Islam, and indeed we improve the quality of the debate. This is without extensive participation in the media: look at the number of writers in the press who have written about Islam and Muslims and check to see how many of them are actually Muslim. Is this why Edward Said chose to begin his influential *Orientalism* with Karl Marx's: 'They cannot represent themselves; they must be represented'?[40]

What about those British Muslims that are fighting with the Taliban? Déjà vu? The same questions were asked during the Gulf War when some British Muslims were interrogated about their loyalties. I would agree with the mainstream, 'If you're going to go, then don't come back.' The stories, true or false, raise the spectre of the enemy within and it is a powerful narrative to argue against. In fact, there isn't much anyone can do, once the label has been fixed. If I deny, then I am told that I am lying, and to accept is to become a traitor. Maybe this is about a drowning nationalism holding on to the nearest scapegoat? As it drowns, it points to the treacherous Muslims: 'Can you not see why you need me?' I am using Bobby Sayyid's argument from his book *A Fundamental Fear*. He suggests that the decentring of Europe permits Islamism to emerge. Taken from the vantage point of the dominant discourse, Islam can be seen as the justification for various discourses that are past their sell-by date. I would suggest that we have witnessed several discourses utilising recent events as opportunities to prop themselves up. These include liberalism, feminism, materialism, and nationalism. Since the voice of Islam is either unheard or unintelligible, these discourses are able to promote their perspectives by holding up a lazy caricature and then shooting it down.

* * * * *

Madness. Civilisation. These words are used to frame our moral discourse because we don't at present have an understanding of the word 'wrong'. The hijackers were mad. What kind of madness was it? Schizophrenia? I think not. When we say mad, we actually mean that we don't know what to say, we don't understand, we cannot categorise them.[41] So they must be mad. To guess at their mind set, I don't think that they were mad. I think that they had become in true twentieth-century fashion numb to suffering. They could see their own death and the death of thousands of others ahead of them, but they had become numb to suffering, perhaps numb to moral discourse. They had heard Western political leaders sidestep the murder of tens, hundreds, or thousands of Muslims one too many times and they had moved from the stage of intense pain to numbness. This is the point at which Islamic law steps in, and holds us back, for I too am numb to suffering. If Muslims are to be critical of themselves, and indeed now they need to be so, they should ask about what has happened to Islamic law that can abandon its traditional self so completely to permit some acts which are so obviously forbidden. I leave this question to those who are more knowledgeable on this than I, but I urge the average Muslim like myself to think about their relationship with the law, because the law is a blessing, it protects us even from our own selves. We are living in times when laws and rules, rights and wrongs, don't mean much. One million people use cannabis every week against the law in Britain and the argument for legalisation is: 'Well, so many people break the law, so let's change it.' Muslims have to be careful that they don't join in. The law is sacred in Islam, as the expression of a divinely-guided consensus. As soon as this is challenged and doors are opened for furious men to re-read the scriptures themselves and ignore the scholars, then we will begin to arrive at destinations that we did not intend.

We are passing through a weak phase in our history and we should not feel the need to defend every Muslim for any action. Unfortunately, some Muslims can do certain things which are not only forbidden in themselves, but can also lead to the dishonouring of Islam and threaten the safety of other Muslims. We cannot say on these occasions that we must defend our co-religionists at all costs. We have to have some moral standards which do not reflect a base nationalism; our ethics have to override our sense of community. In fact, this is what is needed for the whole of mankind. The ulema have all condemned the actions of September 11, and it needs to be understood that if there is a particular way of thinking through Islamic law that can lead to this, then we have to understand it, analyse it and then condemn it also. Of the books on postmodernism and Islam, Bobby Sayyid and Ziauddin Sardar stand out as more thoughtful however Akbar Ahmed does say one thing in his book on *Postmodernism and Islam* which I believe is pertinent to the current Muslim predicament.[42] He says that the media may succeed in changing Muslim character. I believe that they have and to our detriment. Angry, suspicious, closed-hearted, fearful, narrow-minded, ignorant (frankly) and impatient. I know and understand why we have become like this, but I, all praise be to Allah, have moved on, and I urge others to do so. The Muslim scholar and mystic Ibn Ata'illah says in his *Hikam*: 'The source of every single disobedience is being pleased with oneself.' It is time that we recognised our own faults.

The media not only distort character, they also distort our analysis of the situation. Can there be any doubt that our proposed solutions to the Muslim predicament are determined heavily by the media focus upon crisis events, victims and violence? Does this not valorise a political and military solution (hence the rapid rise of such groups during the nineties)?

Instead, the Qur'an says: *'Verily, Allah does not change a situation of a people until they change what is in themselves.'* Perhaps the media makes us conveniently shift the focus away from our own selves, for indeed are we not responsible for our situation? Iqbal's *Jawab-i Shikwa*, written almost a hundred years ago, is perhaps as relevant today as then: 'If you are faithful to Muhammad, then I am yours. This world is nothing, the Tablet and the Pen will become yours.'

I fear that as the situation progresses, we will let the media decide our agenda for us. A similar thing happened during the Rushdie Affair. Muslims began to support Ayatollah Khomeini's fatwa even though Sunni Islam had a different fatwa. Because the media were asking 'Whose side are you on?', many Muslims by jumping quickly through a few logical hoops decided that they were for Khomeini. Similarly, we have to be careful that the media do not push us to argue for positions that are simply forbidden (*haram*). That is, that in order to defend Islam from the accusations of non-Muslims, we decide to take up positions that distort the Islamic perspective.

The last decade or so has seen the increasing radicalisation of the Muslim position, especially within the British national public sphere. This can be demonstrated by referring to the choice representative of national newspapers of 'Islamic fundamentalism'. The first such representative was Kalim Siddiqui who was probably the most radical and strong-minded defender of Ayatollah Khomeini's fatwa during the Rushdie Affair. The second choice representative was Omar Bakri Mohammed, a former leader of Hizb ut-Tahrir and now leader of the al-Muhajiroun faction, who is more ambiguous in his pronouncements but generally against the use of violence. The third is Abu Hamza al-Masri, a spokesman for the Salafi Jihad movement, who is more assertive still and believes in the use of violence. Kalim Siddiqui was popular in the early nineties, though he gave way to Omar Bakri Muhammad in approximately 1993–1994, while Omar Bakri Muhammad gave way to Abu Hamza in the late nineties. All three represent small minority affiliations in the Muslim community. This progressive radicalisation of the

Muslim representative was paralleled by the accompanying radicalisation of Muslim youth after the Gulf War, Bosnia, Chechnya, Kashmir and Palestine. The events of September 11 reversed this process. The death and destruction seemed to be at the hands of Muslims. There was now a tendency towards moderation as many Muslims began to decry the radicalised alternative, 'We must stop this madness!' But the bombing of Afghanistan put a stop to that too.

Reading the media over the last two months or so has made me realise how much the radicals and the Islamophobes need each other. One such Islamophobe, the TV presenter Robert Kilroy-Silk, had decided to focus one of his complex television discussion programmes on the issue of Muslims in Britain fighting against the British alongside the Taliban. Omar Bakri Mohamed had been invited to join the discussion. A campaign (mainly by Muslims) began to e-mail, phone and fax those involved with the production of the programme in order to dissuade them from asking Omar Bakri Mohamed to participate. Eventually the campaigners succeeded, but Kilroy-Silk was furious.[43] I felt while reading his article that perhaps there is a symbiotic relationship between Islamophobes and extremists. They need each other.

* * * * *

There are calls for a Muslim reformation. What do they mean? Where is the Islamic Catholic Church whose authority should be challenged? Is it not the absence of religious authority that has brought us to where we are? So what is meant, demanded, by this call? The last person on earth whom Muslims would be prepared to listen to on such issues is Salman Rushdie, a Pip to modernity's Miss Haversham ('I would do anything to please you, Madam'). Yet he wrote 'Let's start calling a spade a spade...', meaning that this is indeed a war against Islam, and that 'the world of Islam must take on board the secularist-humanist principles on which the modern is based, and without which their countries' freedom will remain a distant dream.'[44] Perhaps

33

this is what is meant by a Muslim reformation: secularism, not scripturalism. But then to what extent should Islam be modified for it to be deemed acceptable? Could somebody please provide a list of all appropriate changes that we should make in order to become worthy citizens of this new moral order? Of course, I jest. Let's call a spade a spade. Islam doesn't need to take on board secular humanist principles, this would never be sufficient, for secular humanists have problems with basic religious beliefs such as God and accountability in the Hereafter. It is not the legal periphery of Islam that is the problem, it is its spiritual centre. As we have seen in Britain, the adoption of such an approach has led to the demise of religion itself.

The call for a Muslim reformation is in one sense a call for a liberal Islam. The subjugation of Islam to the heart's command may provide opportunities for the emergence of liberal Islam, but it is the same hermeneutic that leads to an Islam that advocates violence. Rendering the interpretation of law to the heart's desire may not lead to the desired outcome. In fact, the present political climate tilts the balance heavily away from any conciliatory interpretation of Islam, quite the opposite. But the line that establishes the Western moral position (if there is such a thing) is in a perpetual state of motion. Are all others condemned to play catch up from now on? Or will they be permitted to establish themselves as alternatives? If others are to play catch up, then maybe one way that they could try to break ahead is by asking what is post-post-modernism and making sure they get there first? Ultimately though, Islam has a stronger historical claim than liberalism, having lasted longer while establishing itself across a wider spectrum of cultures. Islam doesn't require a reformation; liberalism needs to de-centre itself.

* * * * *

The cinematographic power of the images of September 11 could perhaps be explained as modernity's hara-kiri. The world watches two planes fly into the Twin Towers on TV through satellite communication. Is this the end of modernity? Is this what is meant by the numerous references to 'the challenge to our whole way of life'? Were the events of September 11 the result of modernity's disregarded children returning to their homes? Or perversely, were they the championing of modernity? That modernity could only be attacked through modernity itself – thus establishing it as the sole surviving grand narrative? That in its moment of supreme weakness, modernity established its universal strength? Or is it all about postmodernism and Islam? How strange that the images on our TVs fluctuate between the city that symbolises postmodernism unlike any other, New York, and the villages of Afghanistan that symbolise the most pre-modern of eras. It is as if the trajectory of progress is being narrated visually. I wonder if bombing Afghanistan would have been so easy if it had been a modern or postmodern country? Or does it make it more difficult? Do their traditionalism and clear Otherness facilitate our bombing? Or does their poverty make us gulp out of shame? Probably both.

About the Taliban themselves and the numerous stories concerning their ultra-Otherness, I am sceptical. Remember the 'babies-in-incubator' story that was employed prior to the first Gulf War to demonstrate Iraqi barbarism, and which later turned about to be false? Politics and the media, already as Siamese twins, tend to merge into one body during war efforts. I remember Malcolm X's comment about the Japanese (or the Germans?) and the Russians, and how the American media so swiftly switched public opinion pre-1945 and post-1945, and wonder whether the same is not happening now. Were the Taliban not welcomed a few years ago by the US embassy in Islamabad as a stabilising force? The numerous photographs, TV footage and eyewitness accounts are to be taken with a pinch of salt. I am not saying that the media lie: they only strategically misrepresent.

Strategic misrepresentation? Let me give you an example. The Ouseley Report published in Bradford in the aftermath of the riots of 2001 was extensively covered in the media.[45] A salient claim was that religious schools in Bradford have led to segregation and in fact are implicitly the cause of the race riots.[46] This point has been repeated again and again, especially as evidence against the government's proposed scheme to expand the number of faith schools, and became a sub-narrative to the September 11 attacks. The report, however, also includes the following points: there is a white flight from 'Asian inner city' areas towards the suburbs, Islamophobia is regarded as prevalent in the schools and community and the police 'collude with non-intervention' in the drugs problem.[47] These points are never mentioned, even in the liberal press. Instead, the blame is laid at the door of the sole Muslim school in Bradford which is supposed to have caused the riots. It is a girl's school. Correct me if I am wrong, but I didn't see any girls rioting. The mass of non-Muslim readers, not knowing any better, would have been content with the story of religion yet again dividing and disrupting society. The truth of the matter is far more complicated, and much less gratifying. The point about Algeria mentioned earlier is relevant here. The denial of freedom in the name of freedom through the distortion of facts is happening in front of our very eyes.

So the Afghanis can taste freedom now. Cinemas, pop music, how could anybody tolerate life with such huge absences? A question that I ask myself is to what extent Afghanistan should approximate to Western cultural practice for the various Western lobbies to be satisfied? (I know, I'm homogenising Western culture.) Polly Toynbee's article 'Behind the burka' in the *Guardian* was an angry critique of the treatment of women in Afghanistan.[48] Reading the article again, it is obvious that her ink must have burnt from the intensity of her hatred. It couldn't have taken her long to write it. Anyway, that evening the television schedule offered the following choices at approximately 11 pm. BBC1: Jo Brand. ITV1: Lily Savage. CH4: Graham Norton. What does this say about gender in Western culture, except that it is somewhere between swings and roundabouts. Perhaps, that's what irks some intolerant feminists so much, that Islam provides a reasonable, working model for gender.[49] Holding up the burka in order to shoot it down helps the intolerant feminist avoid facing the consequences of gender disruption (which have yet to be assessed).

* * * * *

If the key question is: How do we make the world safer, then immediate and obvious answers are: American troop withdrawal from Saudi Arabia, a ceasing of intelligence agency interference in Muslim countries especially in relation to the move towards representative and accountable government, a return of Israel to pre-1967 borders, secure environmental protocols, and fairer global economic trade agreements. Long-term answers relate to shifts in industries reliant upon oil and warfare. Can the world's brains not think up alternative ways of making money? Those who read books know this. But the game of modern-day politics is to avoid the obvious and excuse the inexcusable. I ask myself two questions as I listen to the experts: 'How close do they get?' and 'What excuses will they offer?' The second question is the linguistic equivalent of hide and seek. Self-explanatory? Perhaps these two strategies could be called the strategies of prevarication and containment. A third question that I ask myself is, 'Do they know any better?'

Terrorism is inherently related to fear. The fear of disruption, disorder, chaos. The violation of our structured world, our life, our concerns, our ... Where does this 'our' end? It ends probably where the threat of terrorism begins. A fear of disorder that was realised so spectacularly on September 11. 'Things have changed forever.' Have they? If the US had not bombed Afghanistan, then maybe. But they did. And at that moment Osama bin Laden won the war. A rich man who lives as if he is poor won the war when the richest nation on earth began to bomb one of the poorest nations on earth. So things have not changed. Well, not for the rest of the world, and not for the short term anyway. Long term, things may change. And I think the greatest effect of the events of September 11 on the US has been and will be symbolic. A confident and secure nation will never feel the same way again. The worrying thing is that in post-moral times, the events of

September 11 do provide a strong moral basis for action. But that is all that Western leaders have. And they will need much more if they wish to move beyond rhetoric. I fear as I type that I am typing in vain. Albert Camus said 'If our speech has no meaning, nothing has meaning.'[50] Make no mistake about it folks, this ain't a crusade. It's only an escalation in the cycle of violence. Is losing language worse than losing life?

> The heart ordered the voice:
> 'Hold yourself, until I say',
> And the cynic ran away.

2 The Muslim Condition

What occupies the Muslim mind? As events, chapters and details are all added day by day to an accumulating narrative, I wish to raise a question at this hour: what concerns us? How are we thinking through these various events? Who decides the manner in which we respond? Can we ignore these events? It seems that the language, the manner of response and the analysis are in many senses dominated by the media. It is after all the media that constructs our view of the world on a daily basis.[1] Every day people die and are born, goods are bought and stolen, people make speeches and write books, and all of these events are filtered by those who decide on the extent of newsworthiness such that some of these events are more important than others – that is, they become more available to the public conscience than others.

The first filter is the minute-by-minute newswire of Reuters or the Associated Press, which is itself dependent upon a variety of factors: the close proximity of their correspondent or associate to the event, its relevance to the current narrative canon and the competition of other events that may be viewed as more important. All of these factors at the stage of the first filter decide what ultimately becomes newsworthy. The journey from this point to the *News at Ten* or the tabloid front page is similarly dependent upon similar kinds of decisions and processes at different levels of editorial hierarchy (and their relationships with proprietors and government officials). But this radical contingency is lost in the living room conversation as this heavily-filtered news output begins to confirm prejudice, in all directions, such that the conspiracy is proved true or the universal terrorist threat is affirmed. However, Muslims, like everybody else, have to be careful here because the media can exert such an influence that our whole understanding of reality can become dependent upon media-constructed notions of power and history. History has shown, for example, that all superpowers have withered away, and more importantly, we believe as Muslims that ultimately there is only the One Power, the Source of all Power, the Eternal. The media instead turns our attention away from the Eternal against the purpose of creation towards the variety of perpetual stories in public life. But what is Eternal and what is temporary? Allah is Eternal, and the present situation of our *umma* is temporary.

This chapter is an attempt to answer the question: how can we Muslims get out of our present predicament? I begin with a short discussion on various aspects of the media's depiction of events and our response to them. I then move on to discuss one major consequence of this kind of dialectic: ideological groupings and identity discourse. I then end this chapter by examining the limitations of such discourses and pointing towards what I would wish to suggest as a more authentic expression of Islamic religiosity.

A rock and a hard place: between imperialism and terrorism

Let us begin with the two dominant narratives. The hegemonic position is almost monist in terms of the totalitarianism of its language: it focuses upon the act of violence, the cameras follow the blood of innocents, and the microphones pick up the screams of pain. These real images are allowed to linger as we ask the questions of ourselves, and no framing is required – the perpetrators are depicted as mindless zealots who are locked into forcing violence upon others because that is the way they are and therefore they can only be killed. The subaltern position, however, points to an empire that feels threatened, that knows no legal boundaries, that is continuously rewriting its own rulebooks so that it can ultimately win in whatever game is being played. These are the two competing, dominant languages.

How do these global narratives impact upon a local community? The war on terror has been, in one sense, an attempt to formulate a kind of monism. However, there remains widespread support for various causes throughout the Muslim world including from Muslim communities that are embedded in European and American cities. This monism is forcefully applied upon Muslim communities through the question: 'Why don't you criticise terrorist acts more?' Since these twin hegemonic languages are so diametrically opposed, the subtext to this question becomes: 'Why don't you join our side?' The discomfort that such pronouncements create is not due to some ambivalence towards the murder of innocent people. Usually, a delayed consensus emerges that such acts are forbidden, unjust and wrong. Instead, the discomfort is due to the seeming lack of availability of a third option since there is only terrorism and imperialism. To criticise imperialism is to become a distant relation of the terrorist. To criticise terrorism is to become a distant relation of the imperialist. In fact, there is a certain amount of insanity to all of this – if insanity is the result of the forceful acceptance of two opposites. On the one hand, Muslims are expected to condemn terrorism, and then on the other, the governments of the US and Britain continue with their policies, for example in supporting Israel or invading Iraq. So the cause of terrorism increases, and terrorism is simultaneously more forcefully condemned. What options remain for the oppressed? Here, some Muslims have successfully negotiated the two paradigms to adopt a stance in which they are simultaneously condemnatory of imperialism and terrorism. The present global order would no doubt prefer some of us to take the next step and adopt the Mandela option. Nelson Mandela is regarded as a great figure because he forgave his oppressors – the non-violent victim. His option, although it could also be called the Gandhian option, is championed because the oppressed are not allowed to be violent in today's world. As Bhikhu Parekh suggested through his fictional dialogue between Gandhi and Osama bin Laden, why don't Muslims advocate non-violence? Why do the oppressed disgrace themselves through violence? The answer must surely lie with the oppressed.[2]

Anti-Muslim opportunism and the pills of humility

The events of 11th September have also opened up a window of opportunity to those who wish to peddle populist prejudices and who would have previously been made to feel uncomfortable while doing so; in other words, the boundaries of acceptability have widened. This is because the *zeitgeist* has shifted against cultural relativism as multiculturalism is on the back-foot. For some strange reason, terrorist acts have shifted the whole context of the multicultural debate. Since there is no connection between the topic of integration and the terrorists of 11th September, this can only be regarded as a form of opportunism by those who have never felt comfortable with human diversity. This opportunism is based upon a particular understanding of how people actually change their minds. This approach believes that shaming people is more effective than persuading them. In pursuit of this, some sectors of the media and the academic world are engaged in a rebranding exercise linking Islam with violence, oppression and so on. The simple retort is to add up and compare how many people have been killed by the US military and its allies and al-Qaida and its affiliates since 11th September. This point about historical contingency can perhaps be highlighted by the French *l'affaire du foulard* (headscarf affair) which began in earnest in September 1989 – eight months after the fatwa by Ayatollah Khomeini against the writer Salman Rushdie. A window of opportunity for a climate of prejudice was opened then and the process has repeated itself now in France with its outlawing of all ostentatious religious symbols in public schools in 2004, except that as the French have suggested that Sikhs should wear hairnets instead of turbans, it has repeated itself as comedy.

Jan Pieterse in his book on the history of cultural representation of African-Americans shows that as the anti-slavery argument became more powerful during the time of William Wilberforce, polarizing representations simultaneously became more prevalent.[3] That is, as attempts were made to decrease the distance between opposites, a counter-reaction followed in which the difference was exacerbated. This analysis disturbs the assumed relationship between liberalism and culture because, as certain forms of liberalism attempt to extricate themselves from culture, they simultaneously project images of difference that depend upon a cultural history. Sander Gilman's work is also a testimony to this.[4] This point has an economic slant as well in that the progress of the Muslim community in Britain will involve social mobility and hence, as the class profile for some sections of the community changes, then adverse representations may become an aspect of the resistance to such change. In view of this, we have to be careful about the hatred we may arouse in others and all of the above perhaps explains why the reaction of those who are engaged in critiquing Muslim practice is increasingly paranoid and hysterical. I will return to how we can lessen this tension towards the end of this chapter.

However, a blanket condemnation of the media incorporation, or conversely the lack thereof, of the Muslim voice is now unwarranted. There have been several inroads made into the national and local media since 11th September by spokespersons and academics that represent a positive step forward. However, national figures and faces remain absent, and the most famous Muslims in Britain are probably Abu Hamza and Omar Bakri Muhammad. This indicates the extent to which the whole process has been managed. There seems to be no coincidence that such figures have been promoted within certain sections of the media. This repeated exposure of the exception, as both Abu Hamza and Omar Bakri Muhammad are, as the rule helps to redefine multiculturalism towards a language that firmly places

43

Muslims outside of the circle: honour killings, forced marriages, Islamic terrorism, suicide bombers, female circumcision[5] – and this attempted reification within certain sections of the media needs to be interrogated. But as Bhikhu Parekh suggests: 'The assimilationist pressure sometimes has the opposite consequences to those intended by its champions.'[6] These nodes of difference emerge from a cultural *Weltanschauung* that objectifies and condemns the acts of others as barbaric while privileging the moral life of the self as clean from all these contaminations. But this construction of difference needs to be challenged – at both foundational and rhetorical levels in relation to moral practice. At a foundational level, if we take key discourses upon which modernity is assumed to be defined such as the privileging of rationality and science, the mechanics of democracy, the possibility of liberal individualism and the toughness of nationalism, then those who are familiar with academic musings over the last half-century or so will know that such assumptions can no longer be taken for granted. In fact, they stand as vastly weakened versions of their former selves. Hence, the meaninglessness of their employment in shallow discussions of Islam and modernity. Even Ernst Gellner, who can stake a stronger claim to intellectual competence on these issues than most, could observe that the only reason why modernity was 'right' was because 'it worked'.[7] The point is that the liberal foundationalist hope for moral absolutism can flounder if challenged. For example, one resort for the foundationalist liberal is a Britishness built upon human rights, but this seems to lack insight because, for example, it fails to acknowledge how it can be used to exclude others as un-British or illiberal.

The rhetoric on moral practice is similarly confusing. It is true that suicide bombers kill, but then so do missiles that are fired from fighter aircraft. What two-word appellation do we have for the latter? Similarly, it is also true that some people kill their relatives as a way of preserving their honour, but then so do husbands in British society who found that their wives had been unfaithful – but what two-word appellation do we have for their crime? Female circumcision is condemned because the values of a culture are forced upon the female body, so what of breast enlargement, or more generally, plastic surgery as a whole that seeks to pursue accepted notions of beauty? Polygamy is condemned, but pornography is widespread, and even occasionally celebrated, while the decriminalisation of prostitution is being mooted. It is true that there are many Islamic practices which are un-modern, but while we may not be able to explain every Islamic injunction persuasively, we can take comfort from the fact that those who condemn us most stridently do so from a position that is itself beginning to appear increasingly absurd.

Many of the assumptions that underlie the debate around Muslim integration are in fact barriers to integration themselves – in other words the framing of the debate worsens or indeed creates problems. Why, for example, did the *Guardian* or the *Independent*, as bastions of Enlightenment liberalism, accept Muslims before the *Telegraph*? Is it because anti-racism is more important than the sharing of values? Why is religion as a marker more significant than old age and disability? Does the marking of Muslim religious identity exacerbate Muslim identity politics? Should immigration not affect the society that it impacts upon? Does Islam lead to the empowerment of women in that few things regulate Muslim male sexual behaviour more effectively than the criticism of a pious wife? Are honour killings not better understood as collectivist forms of crimes of possession? Is a Muslim underclass emerging as it begins to be more integrated? In what ways is our experience similar to the Irish experience of terrorism and or the Jewish experience of assimilation? These questions are proposed to confound the many assumptions that underlie the current debate.

What is happening is that we are being forced to try to understand each other, but an important part of this is being organised by those who do not wish to see genuine understanding emerge. Life is complicated, but prejudice only requires a certain amount of knowledge. Easy conclusions on important issues can encourage prejudice – but understanding and analysis has been rare. For example, a generalised Western critique of 'Muslim practices' obliterates the distinctions Muslims make between them: some practices such as honour killing and female circumcision, particularly in its extreme form, are universally condemned and forbidden, some such as 'suicide bombing' are disputed, and polygamy is permitted. But these moral distinctions are not clear to the public conscience, because the force of the rhetoric obfuscates such distinctions.

Perhaps an example would help. Clifford Geertz examines the kinds of individualism two Muslim societies manifest:

> 'Mysticism', 'piety', 'worship', 'belief', 'faith', 'sacredness', 'tradition', 'virtue', 'spirituality', even 'religion' itself all these words we use, as we must, for there are no others by means of which we can talk intelligibly about our subject – thus turn out, when we compare the way in which each our people's came, on the whole, to develop a characteristic conception of what life was all about, a conception they called Islamic, to mean rather different things in the two cases. On the Indonesian side, inwardness, imperturbability, patience, poise, sensibility, asceticism, elitism, and an almost obsessive self-effacement, the radical dissolution of individuality; on the Moroccan side, activism, fervour, impetuosity, nerve, toughness, moralism, populism and an almost obsessive self-assertion, the radical intensification of individuality.[8]

Such deep interpretations may also help in the analysis of gender in Muslim societies. Those familiar with the variety of Muslim cultural life will know that while the public, outward manifestations may be similar, actual private relations may be differentiated and involve alternative notions of masculinity and femininity. What is happening is that the transition of 'Western society' from modernity towards a postmodern unravelling is leading to a situation in which multiple moralities are becoming publicly more available, and not all of them have their gaze firmly fixed towards the future.

Three types of knowing

All of the above is an attempt to outline a sociology of knowledge, and so I wish to distinguish between three different kinds of knowing: knowing of, knowing about and knowing. The first kind is a glancing kind of knowledge: it is the first threshold beyond ignorance. To know of something is to have heard of the subject, but not much more than that. Perhaps a sentence or two on the subject might be all that can be recalled. The second kind is a slightly more elaborate form of knowing: the subject matter is known, perhaps its relations with other subjects are also known, and explanations, attributions, causes, and histories could all be briefly provided. This kind of knowing involves being able to speak about the subject matter for a short while, but no more than that. The third kind of knowing is knowing itself. The subject is thoroughly understood; its history, relations, internal distinctions and so on are all familiar and, if pursued, then this kind of knowing could provide the content for lengthy conversation.

In the main, the media provides the first and second kinds of knowing whereas the third kind, knowing itself, can only be attained through individual study. Since 11th September, the change in popular levels of knowledge about Islam and Muslims is that now many people can talk about Islam and Muslims for about half an hour, but it would be a totally prejudicial conversation – as such shallow or sham forms of prejudice have been fortified. As the media is the main source of public knowledge about Islam and Muslims, we Muslims have little influence or control over what is known about us. In this sense a cultural objectification of Islam and Muslims has developed when in fact it is cultural inclusion that is required. While this cultural objectification does not represent the total trend, it is, however, the most important aspect of the present state of affairs. The only antidote against this social poison is our own personal behaviour – our behaviour communicates, it can confirm or deny superficial knowledge of Islam or Muslims.

Ideology and identity politics

I have only written in a very general way about recent media representation of Islam. I wish to focus however on one consequence, ideology, that is a direct result of this continuous stream of representations. Major events and their depiction almost necessitate ideological responses. This was certainly evident in the early nineties after the First Gulf War (1990-91) and the war in former Yugoslavia (1992-95). It can also be demonstrated by the success of two forms of association within the Muslim public sphere: ideological organisations and charities. Both depend upon the repeated imagery of Muslim victimhood. This may be justified in that many of the world's problems are Muslim-related and that many of the world's victims are Muslims, and that, furthermore, any lack of any response to the suffering of fellow Muslims is surely questionable as it is a sign of faith to feel for fellow Muslims. However, this does not represent the Muslim predicament in its totality, which – with over one billion followers – is extremely complicated and cannot be reduced to a singular narrative of victimhood, especially as William James noted that, 'if hostile to light irony, religion is equally hostile to heavy grumbling and complaint'.[9] That both charities and ideological organisations rely upon such imagery for their success is problematic. Both protagonists would no doubt suggest that such methods are the only methods they have available, but what does the continued focus upon such imagery do to the Muslim psyche?

These ideological groupings are in the main protest movements, and, interestingly, all function in the English language, are based mostly around the campuses, involve a rejection of corruption within the community, specifically amongst the elders, and criticise the lack of religious practice amongst Muslims. The ideological groupings are in essence an 'outside Islam'. A young man views his community on a local and global scale and adopts a vision that takes his focus away from his immediate surroundings towards some complete and global solution to all his problems. This 'outside Islam' even takes the young man's focus away from himself as his criticism focuses on others that have forced this situation upon him.

These groups share a similar philosophical approach even if their conclusions differ. But, having said that, their disagreements have been reduced in recent years. The intense pressure of daily scrutiny and criticism has lead to a peculiar situation in the Muslim community in which Salafis are talking about education, Hizb ut-Tahrir is working on drug rehabilitation, the Muslim Association of Britain has a national, public profile and the Islamic Society of Britain has close relations with the government. One can hear the proverbial bus conductors shouting, 'All change!' What this means is that we are moving beyond our ideological phase – ideology has served its purpose and the demands of a new generation are more exacting as questions are asked as to relevance and utility of political oppositionalism and the cultural isolationism that has, to varying degrees, characterised these groups in the past.

A problem remains, though, in that the sum total of these ideological groupings creates a climate of ideological opinion that becomes fairly resilient to criticism because it is supported across the board. There develops a synergy as well in which this climate spreads its influence to people outside of these groupings. The sum total of this synergy I would label as Muslim identity politics and this lends its colour to the temperament of the community as it mixes with religious adherence in a variety of ways that are almost all negative and inauthentic. This is a kind of temperament that we should question. This returns me to my central question: What is in the Muslim mind? If it is occupied by highly convoluted arguments with suggested anathemas then the words, the facts, figures, rhetoric and feelings will shape the extent of the depth of his religion. This is a form of psychological engagement that privileges the mind and language – and it is shallow religion. The centre of psychological work according to Muslim ontology though is the heart and we are constituted as the self (*nafs*) or the spirit (*ruh*) according to our efforts.[10] Why is this important?

'Inside Islam'

It is important because Muslim identity politics and Muslim character development are two separate and often contradictory ways of working. For example, Muslim identity politics as it manifests itself today is about righteousness, victimhood, anger, pride, the advocacy of self, the blaming of others, the looking out for self and the looking down on others – all of these have been condemned by scholars of the heart. So though it may seem that we are championing Muslim causes, it may be through means that are un-Muslim. Imam al-Ghazali has written lengthy treatises in his *Ihya' 'Ulum al-Din* on the condemnation of anger and pride – both characteristic of identity politics and Ibn Ata'illah condemns self-righteousness and the looking down on others in his *Hikam*. Another problem for the Muslim identity paradigm is its lack of concern for personal morality. Morality in this paradigm is a public matter to be upheld and championed but only on those issues that affect the specific group concerned. This is because, as Iris Marion Young has noted, the nature of public policy dispute forces identity politics groups into cynical manoeuvrings to further their case.[11] But morality, if it is to count in the eternal sense, has to provide a compass for action beyond political posturing, and a personal code that nurtures good character. Islam is therefore not a form of nationalism but an ethics. This affects the immediate outcome as well as people will listen to our complaints about the Muslim situation and our concern for the lack of public morality and accountability and then they will watch us in our everyday actions, and, if they see a discrepancy, then our case will be weakened. If we are calling for goodness and fairness on the global scale, then people will look to see if we ourselves have goodness in our everyday behaviour. This point is sometimes extended to such an extent as to make it unreasonable but the issue here is one of methodology, our chosen trajectory of escape has to accept our sinful nature as part of our condition so as then to work to reduce the discrepancies.

Here we come to the second kind of Islam: 'inside Islam'. Its focus is upon the believer's immediate environment – primarily his self, and thereafter those whom he has to serve and then those whom he should serve if he can. This 'inside Islam' concentrates on the details, the small, regular acts of everyday behaviour – he attempts to secure some order and coherence in his life and thereafter provides whatever service he can in his area of interest or concern to those around him. For most this will be in their immediate vicinity, for some – albeit a minority – this will involve some 'outside' kind of work.[12] All of this community work is service (*khidma*) – he recognises that he is only responsible for that which lies within his scope and ability. He feels the suffering of his fellow brothers and sisters but he also knows that endlessly talking about their suffering and the particulars of their political situation will not resolve the situation – he knows that if he is to be sincere to their suffering then his heart must move his limbs to action towards the general betterment of the *umma*, for, as one of the Sufis said, 'If every man were to mend a man, then every man would be mended'. But all of this moral energy can and must only come from a reorganisation of one's priorities and understandings. All of the above should come about as a result of recognising the true nature of things by distinguishing between that which is miniscule and that which is Magnificent, and by choosing between that which is temporary and that which is Eternal. Once these realities begin to dawn on one, and one submits oneself to the true nature of things, then the rest is merely a matter of following that which is logically obvious.

Ideology, though, only ever has a passing influence as its effects tend to wither with time, and as the real, immediate issues make themselves known. Talking about the *khilafa* makes way for talking about drugs, talking about the details of the Islamic creed (*'aqida*) makes way for talking about education, talking about Islam and democracy makes way for talking about disenfranchised youth, and, even on a personal level, ambition will have to make way for service, and, most crucially, being distant from the Kind and Gentle gives way to a longing and yearning for closeness. The various groups have begun to shed their ideological baggage, and it seems that at present the '*da'wa* scene' is in a state of flux. So how are we to agree on the way forward?

The first point has to be sincerity before the All-Knower. Imam al-Ghazali begins his *Ihya' 'Ulum al-Din* with a stinging critique of religion as industry. There is no doubt that much of what is becoming institutionalised within British Islam is religion as industry – small economies within small fiefdoms. And therefore the nurturing of sincerity at the heart of these small communities will be central to their success.

The second point has to be our refinement, good manners, morals, decorum and decency (*adab*). *Adab* should become the universal Muslim language. It should be the marker by which we can identify each other: the way we talk, the way we look, the way we act: all are indications of the state of our hearts.[13] *Adab* also regulates our disagreements: did we raise our voices? Did we plot against our brother behind his back? In this sense, one measure of our goodness – or perhaps more appropriately, our closeness to the Divine – is our *adab*, even in matters of eating and personal hygiene. All of this regulation of behaviour is ultimately only obedience to the Way (*Sunna*) of the Messenger and a recognition of the Divine Command.

The third point has to be the following of the orthodox legal schools (*madhhab*s). Take two common suggestions: 'I can derive my own law from the Qur'an and the *Hadith*' and 'I want to follow a scholar who does not follow a *madhhab* himself'. The first suggestion rejects *taqlid* or the idea that the unlearned are obliged to recognise authoritative religious scholarship. The second suggestion accepts the necessity of *taqlid* as long as it is to any authentic and well-recognised scholar. The first suggestion is no longer widely regarded as credible.[14] The second suggestion holds some weight amongst some Salafis, but they still have to show how the individual scholars that they wish to follow instead are somehow stronger when lined up against the scholarship of any of the four *madhhab*s. If the Salafis could arrive at a *fiqh*-related meeting point from which they can negotiate their interaction with others without condemnation, then this could open the doors of mutual opportunity.

The fourth point has to be an agreement on the forbidden nature of killing people who are not directly involved in warfare. The *jihadi* argument has extended the limits of permissibility in this area and this perspective has leaked out into other groupings. What is required is the rejection of such points of view and the affirmation of the sacredness of all human life.[15]

The fifth point then has to be an agreement on the problems that face the community. If the starting position is that working on extra-local platforms, i.e. at national and international levels, is for the few and may ultimately remain chimeral, then the focus for the majority of activists – that is those who wish to serve their communities – has to be their local communities. Without wishing to romanticise localism, there can be little doubt that the most effective form of intervention is locally-based. This approach would require the outlining of strategies across major urban areas where those who share similar concerns might identify the key challenges that they wish to take on, and this should be closely followed by regular auditing of the extent of achievement within these projects. In the mainly post-industrial areas where many British Muslims live, this would include an analysis of educational standards, delinquency, employment and health. A simultaneous awareness of avoiding exclusively negative strategies, namely to move beyond victimhood, would help to protect ourselves against a worsening psychology, for example, through volunteering or mentoring schemes, outdoor clubs and artistic endeavours. Essentially, this is about the fostering of an Islam within an urban environment, and I wish to suggest that the response may vary according to class demographics. For example, inner city areas may suffer more from a lack of inclusion whereas more middle class communities may face the challenges associated with assimilation. As the world as a whole moves towards urbanisation, the challenge of making Islam work within a variety of city environments becomes ever more urgent.

The sixth point concerns the level at which organisation becomes abstracted. Many of the organisations have maintained a national focus and this is an indication of the extent to which the parameters and the kinds of categories that we employ are determined by the modernity which many of us have implicitly assumed. Even Hizb ut-Tahrir, the most anti-nationalist of the groups, has a national leadership, i.e. it has a chapter that operates as Hizb ut-Tahrir Britain. But there is no reason why those who are committed to *khidma* have to organise at a national level, or, for that matter, at a regional or local level. They should organise at that level which makes most sense in light of the objectives that they wish to achieve, and it would be my contention that most of what we would wish to accomplish can best be achieved by focusing on individual cities. It is important to note here that ideology becomes more influential as one moves towards the national level of organisation. Otherwise, we should be united in our hearts in helping each other, being generous towards each other, respecting and working honestly with people's specialities and arenas of service. Similarly we should turn away from disliked forms of social activity such as gossip, rumour-mongering, backbiting and pointless conversation – that is, we should account for our time as we account for our wealth. Those who do not adhere to such behaviour should be encouraged to change, as mutually enjoining each other to truth and to patience are two of the four Qur'anic conditions of success.[16]

Barriers to integration

British Muslim communities face four options: assimilation, isolation, emigration or integration. In many senses, these options only remain options to the extent that Muslims themselves are able to achieve them. That is, Muslims cannot integrate themselves, they can only *be* integrated since 'to integrate' in this context can only make sense as a passive verb. In his leaving speech to the Muslim Council of Britain in 2006, Iqbal Sacranie spoke about four significant stages in the development of the Muslim community: mosque building, political campaigning, the formation of the MCB and moving beyond identity politics.[17] I would probably suggest that there are three stages of community development: mosque building (the 1980s), political oppositionalism (the 1990s) and, now – post-9/11 and thereafter – engagement. But, ultimately, while Muslims may seek to engage as much as they wish, they will be integrated only insofar as they are incorporated by powerful 'partner' institutions. If Muslims are to grasp the nettle of integration, it will be the extent to which powerful 'partner' institutions return that gesture through grasping the nettle of Muslim public assertiveness that will determine the success of any attempt at integration.

Tariq Modood sees integration as socio-economic, socio-cultural and civic participation: socio-economic integration is about educational achievement and increasing employability; socio-cultural integration is about the sharing of values; and civic participation is about participation in local and national public life.[18] Civic participation is in many ways up to others, mainly the political parties and the media and more specifically depends on the kinds of representatives they choose to work with. A more open and courageous attitude on both sides will help to increase civic participation immediately and, where this has already been achieved, the results are clear to see. A challenge here for Muslims is the development of a language of engagement that connects with wider society and yet remains truthful to Islamic teachings.

Having outlined the basic parameters for work, I wish to now move on to discuss some of the particulars that affect our manners of engagement in British society. The first point is the style of talking. Political discourse dominates Muslim engagement. The language of rights is prevalent as it mirrors our nationalist concerns. An alternative would be the development of a language of human sympathy that excavates the emotions of everyday life of those who seek the Divine. Instead, our language – the talk of ideology – is the talk of overkill. We jump to condemnations of concentration camps and genocide. The English, however, like to be understated, and in many instances it is worse to be inappropriate than wrong. Another example of the consequences of cultural delinquency is the failure to recognise rhetoric as rhetoric. There is a tradition within the English culture of argumentation that seeks to offend as a matter of provocation – to see how the opposing person will respond. They may not mean what they say, they may simply be attempting to test the robustness of our positions, and so we should recognise their approach as a problem of style and not one of substance. This is to do with norms and codes. British public language operates in codes at the higher and more influential levels. One is expected to understand whether a concession is being offered or to be able to recognise rhetoric as rhetoric.

Another barrier we Muslims face is the rush to theory. Tariq Modood argues that as various cultures and religions have different demands, what is required here is not some universalist multiculturalism for this repeats the mistake of universalist anti-multiculturalism. Instead, what is required is a pluralistic integration that takes into account the various needs of different groups.[19] Another aspect of this rush to theory is how Muslim difference is made absolute, whereas other forms of contradiction are ignored or unacknowledged. This is a form of prejudice. Muslims need to be aware too that their process of engagement with wider society is unlikely to be an easy task, given that there has been some hostility and misunderstanding. We should be prepared to take the rough with the smooth and also be prepared for the eventuality that we may not succeed in every venture, especially at the beginning of this process of engagement.

Thirdly, our method of engagement should be responsive to those from whom we believe the criticism is originating. In the case of the British national sphere, this is mainly the middle classes. And we should remain aware of the origins of the criticisms, especially if the criticisms originate from those who have acted as gatekeepers to wider society for the Muslim community. As such, the language to be attempted is a method of engagement with the middle classes, but the politicised nature of that language means that the middle classes are not positively responding to such attempts. They are far more interested in cultural engagement rather than the rhetoric of rights. Alternatively, the working classes share a rather different outlook and require a different form of engagement. The issues that matter to the middle classes do not raise the eyebrows of the working classes. It is indicative of how far we are from making significant progress that we have failed to develop a useful language for either the middle classes or the working classes. Increasing integration – or increasing equality – could, for example, be adversely affected by the response of the white working classes, who could feel that they are being hard done by when in fact resources are generally being more equitably redistributed. As such, in this context, increasing equality serves to damage integration. This further highlights tensions between law and culture, that is, that an increasing focus towards legal inclusion can be counterproductive and lead to further cultural exclusion.[20] This problem is about relations between communities and it must be addressed by the Muslim community if it is to pursue long-term integration.

One of the reasons why neither the middle nor the working classes are being successfully engaged is cultural illiteracy amongst Muslims. Much of British Muslim engagement relies upon fairly superficial readings of modernity and the present Western condition. This is because many young Muslim activists have mostly pursued careers in the technical, scientific, medical, financial or legal professions, and so they help to work the wheels of British society. There are relatively few Muslim graduates in the humanities and social sciences. One consequence is that our expertise on issues of culture and engagement, one of the foremost issues that we face, remains underdeveloped. In the aftermath of 11th September, we could not muster one expert in American foreign policy from across the whole British Muslim community. By default, the career choices of our best and brightest means that we remain culturally delinquent and are unable to recognise the subtleties required for the art of persuasion.

Even in terms of our immediate urban needs, there are few Muslims who have mastered the trends related to poor educational attainment or spiralling crime, or a sociological know-how of how certain sections of the community are becoming de-educated and more importantly working out how to respond to it. Ideological groupings provide a way out here. They suggest that it doesn't really matter what career path one embarks upon as long as one attends the irregular weekend gathering or the weekly meeting. So if one young man decides that he wishes to contribute to changing his situation and then approaches an ideological organisation, he is then told – at the moment when ideology asserts itself – that he should ignore his immediate situation and focus instead on whatever diagnosis the group is offering. This way, as long as we continue to gather to discuss the problem, while remaining a part of the capitalist architecture within our working lives, then the problem will eventually be resolved – or so ideology promises. The reverse is that we have to begin to choose those career paths and develop those institutions that are more deserving of our life commitment as Muslims. What is required, therefore, is institution building and investment in cultural capital. By this I mean the whole cultural nexus: scholars, intellectuals, historians, artists – that provide some substance, explanation, meaning and expression in a deep and relevant manner, in mass culture and in high culture, to a Muslim presence in Britain. The state or law itself cannot enforce belonging. Belonging or sharing requires persuasion and this lies squarely within the realm of culture, not of the law.

Another consequence of cultural delinquency is the categorical condemnation of all others as enemies: 'We can't work with anybody'; 'They are all disbelievers anyway'; or 'Everything is controlled'. Even amongst ourselves, we Muslims cannot work with the majority of our fellow believers, because some of them do such and such or the others are like such and such. This is again a problem that plagues the manner of our present engagement, although again there are signs that it is changing.

What most of us need to recognise is that of all the non-Muslims, very few are actually completely anti-Muslim. Perhaps a similar number are Muslimophiles who don't know which Muslims to approach or how to approach them. And most are confused, unsure, as they have some misinformation provided to them by the media, but are willing to hear the other side and even change their minds. The refusal by many Muslims to engage, perhaps out of shame or a lack of know-how, means that we have few partners. This has meant that some sections of the left have gone over to the right, whether this is in the form of journalistic commentators or votes for the British National Party. The reasons for this can be summarised from much of the above. As we constantly claim our rights in pursuit of further inclusion, we are in fact becoming further excluded since our claim to legal inclusion is leading to cultural exclusion. It is my main contention that we need to change our manner of engagement from a language of identity-based rights towards one that seeks to further human conversation, to extend human sympathy, and this can only be done through a non-ideological Islam that ignores the daily media frenzy – that is, through deep religion, by means of an 'inside Islam'.

3 A Marcher's Song

Another day, another march, life continues. I had previously decided against marching. But this march looked like it was going to be huge, and I wanted to be there. So I woke up on Saturday 28th September 2002, and made my way to the mosque in central Bradford from where the coach was leaving for London. Having decided at the last minute, I was not booked on to the coach for the more organised, those with nicely-ironed white, flowing robes and packed lunch boxes. No, we had to settle for a minibus which had been arranged for late-comers like me. A box-shaped fifteen-seater, it didn't look like it would make it to London and back, the seats were hard, the engine far too noisy, but there was leg room, this being important for long journeys. My companions on this journey were a couple of religious lads, sitting behind me, a recently reformed ex-convict, sitting opposite me, and three 'rude boys' sitting at the back. At the front was the driver, Hafiz Saheb (someone who has committed the Qur'an to memory), and behind him his younger brother or cousin, and next to them an old man with a white turban and *shalwar kameez* (whom the rude boys had decided to name 'Osama') and his nephew.

So the journey began. We were soon on the M1. I started on my light reading: Camus's *The Myth of Sisyphus* and Nietzsche's *Beyond Good and Evil*. The others began to talk. After a while, maybe near Sheffield, one of the rude boys, moved up to sit opposite me. Taz, as he was known to the others, was studying computers at Manchester Met. He didn't seem like he was the practising type, but he knew some friends of mine in the Islamic society there. He asked me about the books.

'What are you reading?'

'This is a book by Camus and this by Nietzsche.'

'What's it on?'

'Well this one is about the meaning of life, it's by a French philosopher. This one is on morality by Nietzsche, a German philosopher.'

'But what, are they Muslims?'

'No.'

'So why...'

'It's interesting...'

'Isn't it all *kufr*?'

'...what do you mean?'

'I mean, it's just all *kufr*, isn't it? What's the point of reading books like that? At the end of the day, they're all the same.'

'Well, parts of Camus and Nietzsche are in agreement with Islam, I find them useful.'

'Like what?'

'Like for example, Nietzsche criticizes the search for objectivity in the human sciences and that makes sense to somebody who can see that the social sciences needed to be objective if they were to fulfil their historical role as replacements for religion.'

Taz looked down, confused, 'It's all *kufr*, bro.'

'So why march?' He looked puzzled. 'Why march, if it's all *kufr*.'

'I have to do something, man. It's not right, this war business. But I don't think it's going to change anything. So why are you going then?'

'I can't stay at home, it's the least I can do. Maybe if enough people go, the government will change its mind.'

'You joking! This march ain't gonna change anything, bro. It's all set up, cooked.'

'Conspiracy?'

'Course, what, you don't think they're against us?' He looked at me, realized that I didn't. 'Course they are, bro. Everything's cooked, they're gonna deal with Saddam, bro. It's been planned for ages. Then, they're going to move on to Iran, then Syria, then...'

I could see an argument looming on the horizon, I thought for a bit about the rest of the journey, all the way down the M1 and back up again. Did I want to get into an argument at such an early stage? Here we go.

'So who's behind the conspiracy then?'

'The disbelievers...'

'All of them?' He looked surprised at the ease with which I bypassed his allegations.

'Yeah, all of them.'

'Every single one of them?' He nodded. 'Okay, when you say conspiracy, what do you mean.'

'Look at the media, against Muslims, books, against Muslims, politicians, against Muslims...'

'Who says?'

'I says.'

'Have you checked?'

'What?'

'I mean, when you say media, what do you mean, all newspapers and television?'

'Course.' He knew he was on shaky ground.

'Books, publishing houses...'

'Course, look at the books against Islam...'

He looked back at me, unsure, he went for the strongest point he had. 'Look at Israel, no one says a thing. How did that happen?'

We argued about conspiracy theories. I told him what I thought of conspiracy theories, how they're so convenient, how they forfeit any form of engagement, how they simply aren't true. 'If you believe in them, you don't have to do anything, cos, ultimately they will always be in charge.'

We stopped at Leicester Forest East, this was the first indication for the size of today's march. The minibus turned the corner, and a line of coaches became visible. Never has a line of coaches looked so beautiful! Hundreds of people were walking around with their placards, leaflets, scarves. The signs were good. We rejoined the motorway.

The conversation with Taz continued, we moved from the global to the local. The police station built on Lilycroft Road in Bradford, before any major riots, but built like a fortress, as a challenge, an insult, a forewarning.

'Why did they build that police station then? To control us, us and them, that's their mentality.'

'I don't know why they built it.'

'Who decided?'

'Don't know.'

'So why, if they're so kind and nice, why did they build that police station?'

I was stuck, and he was glad, he looked around for more examples. 'Okay, why do they always move away, saying we don't wanna integrate. We moved into Heaton about five years ago, no Pakis on our street, they all moved out, one by one. No one came round to see us. We spoke to them, they didn't to us. So who wants to integrate. Now they're all in Bingley, scared we're gonna move there. Why, cos they don't wanna know us. I'll tell ya something, my dad yeah, my dad....'

'Okay, okay, I know, I know. But it's more complicated....'

'What?'

'You know, self and other err.... us and them. It's to do with otherness, cultural representation....' By now, the other two rude boys at the back had become interested and I tried to talk to them as well, but unlike Taz, they seemed to be present but distant. After a while, it became clear that they didn't understand some of the words I was using, not just the jargon, but sometimes just longer words. They were interested in our conversation, but couldn't participate. Their eyes betrayed their eagerness to join, and their faces the sadness that they couldn't. Ten years at the local comprehensive.

Taz returned to the back of the minibus.

I turned to face the front, and began to relax. But the two religious-looking guys behind me were deep in animated conversation. The one on the left, Saj was listening to a cassette from a series on the life of the Prophet by Imam Sulaiman, an imam from California. This cassette series had recently become extremely popular, an exposition of the life of the Prophet as it mattered and held meaning for a Muslim. The discussion was about his statements after 11th September. He had completely condemned the terrorist attacks. The other lad, Tof, seemed to be a sympathizer with Hizb-e-Siyasi, a political-religious organization that commanded a large following on British campuses in the early to mid-nineties but has since become marginal, though vociferously so.

The early to mid-nineties were a time of great debate between Muslim youth organizations, with at least three were vying for pole position. The oldest was the Muslim Youth Movement, a social-political organization that began in the mid-eighties mainly as a proselytising effort. The second was the Movement for Clarification of Islamic Essentials, a group aligned with reformist-Salafi tendencies emanating out of Saudi Arabia. The third was the Hizb-e-Siyasi, which owed its success mainly to its then charismatic leader – Sheikh IBM (as he was then known) who subsequently left the organization and formed his own, the Musafirun (the Travellers). Imam Sulaiman had appeared on the scene after spending a decade in the Middle East. Converting to Islam in his youth, he had travelled extensively across the Muslim world studying with Islamic scholars, especially in the Maghreb. Eloquent and articulate, and speaking about Islam in a kind of language that was unheard of, he entranced the hearts of many Muslim youth. The confusions that were derivative of being raised within parallel and overlapping cultural, moral and linguistic universes, the inability to articulate a reasonable position from within the Islamic *Weltanschauung*, all these problems made the mental room of young Muslim minds very dark, among the few rays of light that began to brighten up this room were the work of Imam Sulaiman. The other groupings became side attractions over time, but they were waiting for their moment, and 11th September was that moment.

'Why did he speak so well of America? Why doesn't he criticize them for what they're doing in the Muslim world? It's an empire and he's defending it.'

'He's not defending it. He's said many things against America.'

'I didn't hear him, he should say clearly what they are doing...'

Being someone who benefited from Imam Sulaiman, I could only listen for a short while before I turned round, argument number two.

'As-salamu alaykum.'

'Wa alaykum as-salam.'

'Brother, why are you giving him such a hard time.'

'It's not what I want, bro, it's what the Sharia says.'

Normally, I'm quite polite, but this guy had annoyed me. 'What does the Sharia say?'

'You have to speak out against the tyrant.'

'He has spoken out, enough times, what do you want him to say?'

'He hasn't said enough.' We eventually returned to conspiracies. He went through his list of proofs.

'Okay, look, what do you want him to say, that America did this, did that over the last 30 years, we know all this, he knows this, everyone knows this. Are they gonna listen to us when we speak like that? Would you listen to somebody if they spoke to you like that? You wouldn't. What we have to do is speak in a language that they understand and appreciate. No one wants to be spoken down to. Especially by Muslims who are supposed to be backward etc. So you have to make your points in a way that people will listen, you have to give them some space to move, if all you're saying is, 'You're evil, and you are wrong!', then, what do you expect the other person to do but defend themselves? But that's how you want him to speak. You're in a corner, and you want to take us all there....' I paused, he was quiet. 'You can't expect people to come to exactly where you are, but this is what you want, all or nothing. No! You have to give people space to move maybe 10%, maybe 60%, but you need to give room, you need to speak in a way that relates to them. Imam Sulaiman quotes Shakespeare, he says in Shakespeare sometimes you don't know who's the hero and who's the villain and they understand what he is saying, but we are dumbfounded, so why does he quote Shakespeare? Cos he's trying to convince them, not us.'

'Why can't he quote the Qur'an and the *hadith*?'

'He does, but what? You want him to only quote the Qur'an and the *hadith*? Give the guy a break, he is doing more to explain our concerns than Hizb-e-Siyasi is, he is helping our political situation more than they are, they are making enemies for us cos of the way they talk, why? Why are they doing that? If people are willing to listen to you, then why use a language and quote stuff that people don't understand and worse puts them off, they think you're loony tunes or thick or something. Why?'

'Yeah, but...'

I'd had enough. 'He has made more people understand our position than HS ever did. I know that. You know that.' I don't know if I had convinced him, or that he was just too scared to continue the conversation. I was upset, I didn't like the way he spoke about Imam Sulaiman. Tof started practising last year, he didn't know his Qadi Abu Bakr ibn 'Arabi from his Sheikh Muhyiddin ibn 'Arabi, but he knew that he could criticize Imam Sulaiman. Allah save me from the zeal of the newly-practising.

We approached London, and I thought about the contradictions of it all, the conspiracy theories, the refusal to engage, the inabilities, and yet we were all heading to this march, engaging. Osama (the old gentleman at the front who had been named so) had been talking to the driver most of the way down. It was time for Zuhr prayer, we said that we should make our way to the march first and we could pray in central London somewhere, but Osama wasn't having it, so we went to Regents Park Mosque, prayed and then made our way to Hyde Park. The minibus was parked a few hundred yards from the Serpentine

Gallery and we made our way across the park to catch a tube to the beginning of the march.

We joined the march under Big Ben outside Westminster Tube Station. It was packed, huge, surprising, glorious. We walked round the barriers and joined the march, walking slowly. The others broke away, but we were to meet back at the minibus at about six. I walked by myself. Looking across the marchers, I couldn't believe my eyes. I took out my *misbaha* (rosary beads) and began to thank Allah again and again. Once a regular activist, I have been on many marches in my life from the anti-Rushdie march through the Gulf war, the war in Yugoslavia, several Palestine marches and others. We have always been isolated, politically. This was different. We were the minority, overwhelmingly so, and it felt great.

All the way through the march, people were smiling, but serious. I remembered how the Prophet said even a smile is charity. I remembered the stare an old gentleman (who was sitting with his wife) had given me and my wife once at Leicester Forest East as we had walked across the restaurant floor, his eyes emotionless but intent had followed us as we walked the 20 yards. I ignored him, but never forgot him. The impoliteness, the transgression. Or how a friend, who used to send his daughters to a private school, and was ignored by all the other parents for years when he used to go and pick his daughters up, except immediately after 11th September, when they all said without fail 'Good morning'. Or how an academic colleague once very forcefully told me that I was a British Muslim, and that nobody could take it away from me. But she was from abroad and I had been raised here, so who gave her the right to tell me where I was from, except cultural convention? But today, against all these unhappy memories, they smiled at me, and I smiled back. Worcester man, Woking woman, whatever meaningless category the pollsters could conjure up, they were there and they were smiling at me. They knew who I was, what I believed in, what I was about, and they were at ease with it. Even on shaking hands with the opposite sex. I met a friend who was one of the doctors assigned to look after any emergencies and shook his hand, standing next to him was another doctor, I moved on and shook his hand, standing next to him, a third person, a volunteer lady, I didn't know what to do, I held my hand back and placed it over my heart and smiled, I was desperately anxious that she wasn't offended, and she just smiled back, and I moved on. No explanations, just understanding, and a bit of space.

We turned towards Downing Street and the march became congested as the demonstrators slowed down opposite the Prime Minister's residence, to have a good look and in some cases a good shout. The police presence here was at its most visible. Didn't they understand that we were trying to save their relatives from flying off to some distant land in order to sacrifice their lives for someone else's interests? Up towards Trafalgar Square, I cut across to the pavement in order to get ahead of a raucous bunch of rude boys who had started to gather in front of me. They were the usual conglomeration of hoods, labels, trainers, goatee beards, attitude, one-upmanship and aggression. Laughing and joking amongst themselves, once they turned their attention outwards, they took on an angry demeanour. Shouting and swearing in English, Urdu, Punjabi and Arabic. Happily, most didn't understand them. Some of the shouting was far-fetched, some irreverent, some offensive and some just meaningless. I walked past a man on the pavement who was looking on.

'Hello, how are you?'

'I'm fine.'

'Do you know what we're marching about?'

'Yeah, I'm with you guys, but who are those idiots? They'll put people off.' He pointed to the rude boys, I nodded and shrugged my shoulders. I talked to him for a bit and then continued walking. Why were they shouting? Who were they shouting to? The buildings on Piccadilly? I thought back to the brothers on the minibus, how they couldn't join the discussion between me and Taz. How they would be exhilarated here, by all this shouting. The defiance, the turn-around: 'We can answer back, we have a reason to, we are not completely out of the circle, yet.' It was the kind of communication that they had been reduced to, it was the only part of civil society that they could engage in, they didn't need to articulate themselves or know the right words, or construct their sentences properly, they could shout, in their own language if they wanted, and they were communicating, if only to the buildings. A TV camera placed in front of them brought not reasoned argumentation, but jeers and shouts.

But what was the point of shouting? Why don't we just keep quiet and express our disapproval through disciplined silence. 'Down, down USA, Bush, Bush, you will pay.' 'Bush, Bush, we know you, your daddy was a killer too.' 'Come on Tony, get off your high pony.' I couldn't figure out what was the purpose of this attempt at communication, except perhaps a weak sense of momentary power?

But I admired them as well, they were standing up for something. The decimation of many inner-city economies has brought with it a cultural transformation: where there was a work ethic, there is now nihilism, inner-city style. It is not bourgeois, fanciful and ineffectual: it is the result of the breakdown of, in some cases, all moral order. An individualism, an anomie, that Durkheim and Nietzsche warned against. But these rude boys had not fallen into that lifestyle. They were here because they had a sense of justice, of right and wrong, and this was admirable.

But, I wondered as well, was this because of a sense of right and wrong, or in pursuit of a nationalistic sentiment? Was there a moral theory, a theory of justice, a concern against suffering across the board, or was there solely a concern for one's community? Am I asking too much of them? The lack of any obvious ethical theory made me think that this was more nationalism than ethics, and this worried me. I remembered the story of Sayyiduna Ali, the fourth successor to the Prophet. How, in the thick of battle, having just defeated his enemy, he walked away from him because he had spat in his face and this had inclined him towards revenge. His control, his subservience of his self to the principle for which he fought, his chivalry, this is absent today.

Just past Piccadilly I met an old friend, Qasim. We had been together in the Muslim Youth Movement, and both served on the main organizing committee during our undergraduate years. I had since left, partly because I was no longer young, and partly because of Imam Sulaiman's critique of our way of going about things. Qasim had remained and moved onto one the mature equivalents of MYM, of which he was one of the leaders, and now, one of the organisers of this march behind the scenes. He was walking towards Hyde Park, so we decided to walk together – it had been a few years since we last met.

'So what are you up to these days?'

'I'm working as a junior doctor, in Kent. You?'

'Just finished the PhD at Leeds, thinking about what to do next.'

'I heard you were in Fez.'

'Yeah, I've been there for a few months, going back soon, trying to learn Arabic.'

'How's it going?'

'Hard, but the scholars are good, bright. They're teaching Sufi books as well. And you?'

'Just working, and helping out with this sort of thing whenever I can. How is it, I mean, how is it compared to what we used to do?'

'It's very different. They're just different, you know, you read about spirituality in the books, and you're not sure what they mean, but some of the scholars, they're a living embodiment of it, and you begin to understand what it's all about. Before, we used to say that the problem is with everyone else, now we say the problem is with us. Ibn Ata'illah said: "The tear of the sinner is more beloved to Allah than the arrogance of the righteous man".'

'No, I've heard some of the cassettes from Fez and they've helped me. But I still think that the political is the most important: you have to be involved in society, you have to change things. Look, at this march, it's so important now after September 11 that we are on the ground.'

'I don't think anyone is talking about isolation, but "Call yourself to Allah before you call others", that's all.'

'But you weren't exactly...'

'I was messed up, confused, full of nasty emotions, the worst thing is you think that politics, power, the material are the most important things but they aren't, Allah is. It's like society or the media takes the place of Allah, cos that's all you think about. It's what's in your mind that counts. We need to look to Eternity, to Allah'.

Qasim was quiet, he knew that I was sensitive on this, so we decided to change the topic. Qasim was amongst the more thoughtful of the MYM bunch, and we used to have good discussions and sometimes arguments, but we remained good friends, working closely on campuses which was our remit for work, coordinating campaigns and activities across universities. I thought to ask him about our lack of engagement in British society.

'You know when I think about what happened in the early nineties, all those arguments about *'aqida* (creed) and gradualism, I wonder sometimes, how far off track we were. No-one concentrated on interacting with non-Muslims.'

'I think the problem was that those who were doing so, were doing it so badly, it put us all off. Whatever you say, Islam is, you want Islam to be pro-democracy, we'll make it so, you want Islam to be left-ish, we'll make it so, you want Islam to be green, we'll make it so. I mean I was fed up with those guys, they were just trying anything. It was desperate. Most of us looked elsewhere.'

'I mean all the intricate stuff between us and the HS lot, what use is that now, it was a complete waste of time, all the arguments with people about *ahad* hadith with brothers who didn't even know Arabic, all the detail about the Deobandi–Barelwi issue, I mean the D-B stuff, it's not even an Ash'ari–Maturidi issue, it has no meaning to any Muslim outside of the sub-continent, but everyone knew the issues in detail, and now we need to communicate, to build the bridges that we ignored, and no-one knows how. That's where I think Imam Sulaiman is really providing some answers, it's not just about speaking in English, it's also about knowing how to use the words, about knowing what they mean to others, about the differences in

71

meaning, about trying to get people to understand at least part of where you're coming from. No-one else is doing it. I think that's why people are giving Imam Sulaiman a hard time, he's doing what they just can't understand, but I'm telling you, he's doing something crucial. But most of our lot, don't understand, they never read, hardly speak to anyone, outside of ideological stuff.'

'Ideological stuff?'

'Yeah, you know, their group's material, the cassettes, books, etc. and everyone knows the arguments, but we don't know how to engage. I think most of these inter-group debates, if we were to talk about them with non-Muslims, they'd think we've lost it. We have a highly-developed internal or private language, you know, between ourselves, and a hardly-developed public language, and then we wonder why they don't understand, why we're isolated, I mean... .'

Qasim was listening, every now and then his walkie-talkie would buzz and he would answer it, but then come back. He knew he wouldn't see me again for a few years if we separated. He might have been listening because he wanted to implement these ideas in his group, but I didn't care as long as they were implemented.

'So what are you saying?'

'I'm saying that the ideological phase is over, the Gulf War and Bosnia provided fertile ground for ideological movements in the early nineties when all these groups emerged and fought over intricate details on campuses and in the inner cities, but we've now moved beyond that, we have to, because we're in a post-ideological phase, where those issues don't count anymore, they're irrelevant, and we need to engage with society.'

'Yeah but there's issues, I mean a lot of brothers are saying they're not sure about living here anymore?'

'Well, they need to make some decisions, I think they haven't got the guts to go back, and they want to stay here, yet they don't feel secure, so they can't make a decision, but they have to. There's three questions, first of all, is there any benefit for us to stay here for Muslims as a whole, I think there is, otherwise Britain would be disconnected from the Muslim world, and that would be dangerous. Secondly, can we work alongside people we don't agree with completely, I mean, this is just an irrelevance, cos does anybody agree with anyone 100%? If you follow this question through to its logical end, then everyone will stand alone or within such ideologically-tight institutions that breathing would become difficult. Thirdly, how should we interpret and act upon eschatology and predestination. The *hadith* is that even if the Trumpet for the Day of Judgement is blown, and you're planting a tree, then you should continue to plant that tree, meaning, it doesn't matter what's going to happen from an eschatological point of view, you should still do what you're supposed to do. The guys use this in the same way they use conspiracy theories, as an excuse to do nothing and complain. That's the path of isolation.'

'Yeah, but who's gonna work on this language stuff?'

'This is the problem, look at all the brothers: Ahmad, Sohail, Imran – all medics; Tariq, Taqi, Ismail – engineers; Shehzad – computers. Everyone's gone into the sciences, but how many have gone into the humanities? Every single one of these guys is bright, some exceptionally so, but what are they doing? They're manning the posts, keeping the ship above water, but who's steering it? We don't know. So many people are writing and talking about Islam and so few of us can respond. We know jack about the West, its history, culture, philosophy, politics, literature and we want to live here. Ideas, *adab* (culture), we don't pursue them, and we don't understand someone who does. Then we wonder how to respond to allegation after allegation against Islam. To be honest with you Qasim, and you know I'm not talking about you, most of the guys who take up careers do so cos they wanna climb the ladder. Sorry, but it's true. All these medics, they say they wanna care for people, how many of them have volunteered their services for Médecins Sans Frontières? Jack have.'

'But what do you think about the Islamic movement? Don't you think that we need to work with the Islamic movement?'

'Well, I'm just no longer convinced by the Islamic movement. I think their focus is too much on the state itself and especially government. But what I think they don't realise is that so much of what Islam demands of us today as an *umma* doesn't need the state. I think the Islamic movement has failed to understand the role of the state in the modern world or perhaps they have an understanding that is very close to communism, which is that the state should carry the social burden. I don't see how this can be true except in a limiting, regulatory way. What are the big problems in Muslim society? We have mass illiteracy even in urban areas, major problems in public health and high rates of disability. I mean, have you seen how disabled people are treated in the Muslim world? They have to beg. I remember walking past a person in one of the capital cities and they had to beg to live. That would be unheard of here, it would be a scandal. Look at public health and clean water, our main charities spend much of their time dealing with crises, but we need to shift towards mass public health programmes to keep people healthy. Islamic movements tend to focus on the government itself but power and the ability to change society and improve conditions is not solely located in the state. In fact, the state in many Muslim countries remains a weak institution. Social movements if developed properly can really tackle these problems more than any government can. Here, government after government talks about the importance of the third sector to help the government achieve its aims in what is a fairly well-developed country whereas in the Muslim world they are seeking to capture the state to help them with things that they already have some influence over. I think that one of the problems with Islamism is that it is intrigued by modernity, to such an extent that it cannot see its limits and, more importantly, how it can actually help the Muslim situation right now without requiring the leverage of the state.'

'Are you talking about post-Islamism?'

'Yeah, I think the Islamic movements can achieve many of their objectives by functioning as civil society institutions working to hold the state to account and serving the needs of the weak and poor. In Britain, I can't see what help the Islamic movements bring to our needs here. We have massively different challenges and I don't know how what was written in the 1940s in Egypt and Pakistan now applies here to Britain in Manchester and Birmingham. Our problems are very different – cultural isolation, political disenfranchisement, educational underachievement, identity discomfiture – and we do need a political vision but not one supplied by people who were responding to very different circumstances. The challenges that we face here and that future generations will face here need a different kind of leadership. It's time to move on.'

We started to arrive at Hyde Park and Qasim had to find some of the other volunteers. We hugged and parted company. Everywhere you could look there were people, protesting, demonstrating, and then there they were: the HS had turned up, complete with colour co-ordination (orange this time). I walked past them, nodding to a few memories from the past (we used to argue for hours in Student Union canteens), up to the crowd sat in front of the speakers' stadium. The speeches were as expected, atmosphere-raising, more slogan than sense, but we were here, almost half-a-million of us, and the point had been made. I made my way back to the minibus, and met the others. We prayed 'Asr and departed.

The minibus was facing south, and we joined the traffic at 6pm. I expected Hafez Saheb to turn the minibus round at some point as Osama was directing him. I waited for a bit, then shouted out,

'Hafez Saheb, the M1 is the opposite way.'

No-one moved, as if I hadn't spoken. The rude boys starting looking around, asking me if I was sure, I told them that I had lived near here for a year. I gave it a few minutes and then spoke, 'Err, Hafez Saheb, we're going the wrong way, you need to turn round.' Again no response, both the Hafez and Osama continued looking forward. I gave them the benefit of the doubt, *husn al-zann*, as it is referred to in Islamic literature. Maybe they were going around Hyde Park to drive up Park Lane. No. We crossed the traffic lights, drove past Imperial College and

South Kensington Tube Station. I was annoyed, but decided to wait: maybe I wasn't being patient enough. The rude boys began to look at each other.

After about half-an-hour, we were deep into Fulham, Osama was still giving directions, pretending that he knew the way. The rude boys' looks had turned into quiet murmurs. Eventually, deep in some flash residential area, Osama decided to admit some ignorance. Hafez Saheb turned the minibus around. The murmurings turned into mutterings, and the occasional expletive. Back on the main road, Osama got out and asked some helpful people in the middle of Fulham about directions towards the M1. They obliged, though it was a perplexing, hilarious sight. Admittedly, I had started to see the humorous side of this escapade a while earlier: what could I do? I was stuck between Osama and the rude boys. We saw an empty coach, from Brighton I think, heading towards the park to pick up its allocated proportion of demonstrators. We decided to follow it. About 8pm, we pulled up at Hyde Park. The rude boys were now openly and loudly swearing and cursing.

The minibus pulled up at the top end of Hyde Park, near Speaker's Corner. It had been two hours since we set off from the other end of Hyde Park. Most of the coaches had departed, but there were still a few die-hard radicals distributing their newspapers or leaflets. We were late for Maghrib prayer, so we decided to pray first before setting off. We found a spot near the edge of the park and prayed that we would get home in the same evening. As we walked back to the minibus I saw someone I thought I recognized, Dave, a fellow sociology postgraduate from Leeds. I hardly knew him, though we covered similar areas of work.

'Dave?'

'Hey, Atif, how are you?'

'Fine, what are you doing here?'

'Same as you, marching.'

'I didn't realize you were the marching type.' He ignored my comment. 'How are you getting home?'

'I dunno, I think I missed my coach.'

'So how are you gonna get home?'

'I dunno, maybe they haven't gone yet.' I looked around, there were hardly any coaches left.

'I think it's probably gone, you know. Why don't you come with us? We've got spare seats.'

He thought about it for a short while and then nodded, we walked back towards the minibus, 'How come you guys haven't set off yet?' I kept quiet. I introduced him to the others on the minibus and he sat opposite me. But first we had to get to the M1.

We approached the Marble Arch roundabout, 'Hafez Saheb, if you want to get to the M1, then take that road over there. It's straight all the way to the end.' I pointed to the Edgware Road. Osama kept quiet, Hafez Saheb listened. We turned onto the Edgware Road, and I breathed a sigh of relief. The rude boys were murmuring. We continued up the Edgware Road, past Maida Vale, and entered Kilburn. Osama remarked: 'I don't see any signs for the M1?' The rude boys responded vociferously and offensively. Osama didn't reply. 'Hafez Saheb, it's about another couple of miles.' We continued on the same road. We stopped in Cricklewood at Kebab Full Stop, a nice little take-away that served a variety of kebabs. My popularity in the minibus was soaring. We headed off again. Osama couldn't resist another comment, but the rude boys were not having any of it. Hafez Saheb wasn't so sure, 'Are you sure this leads to the M1?' 'Yes, another five minutes.' He took me at my word. It was approaching 9pm, and we were still in London. He was tired and he still had to drive all the way back. The roundabout for the A406 arrived and we turned right onto the roundabout for the M1. Osama proclaimed loudly and with a surety that betrayed his ignorance, 'Now I remember!' At this point, his nephew, who had been maintaining a graceful silence out of family loyalty, erupted. A hundred words came out so quickly that we could barely understand them, but I think he was criticizing Osama's knowledge of London. As we joined the M1, I put my head back and slept, hoping that I would wake up somewhere near Wakefield.

I woke up, and looked out of the window, waiting for the next motorway sign, hoping for a 34 or a 36, it was 10. We hadn't even got to Luton. I looked across at Dave, he seemed comfortable and not too nervous. I think he had realized why we had set off so late. No one had spoken to him, so I started.

'How's the thesis coming along?'

'It's alright. I'm writing up, should be finished within the year.'

'What's the topic again?'

'I'm looking at the structure of postmodern forms of moral, public reasoning.'

'Who are you using for that?'

'Mainly Berger and Luckmann, but others as well.'

'Sounds interesting, look forward to reading it.'

'What are you reading there?'

'These, Camus and Nietzsche. I read these years ago, wanted to read them again.'

'They must give you a hard time, being religious and that.'

'...In fact I came to Islam after reading them.'

'How's that then? I thought they both asserted the freedom of the individual.'

'Well kind of. They helped me think through liberalism and I think if one takes their critique seriously there can only be suicide or religion, i.e. non-meaning or meaning. I think the appropriation of them as anti-religious tends to obscure the subtleties of their positions, which accepted the power of religious explanation through the meaningless that is a consequence of its absence. I went straight to Islam after reading them.'

'Come on, are you saying that both Nietzsche and Camus are pro-Islamic?'

'No, but ... I had marked the books, and began to flick through them to find the relevant passages. Okay, on the importance of the meaning question, page 4, Camus says: "I see others paradoxically getting killed for the ideas or illusions that give them reason for living (what is called a reason for living is also an excellent reason for dying). I therefore conclude that the meaning of life is the most urgent of questions." On the importance of seeking meaning, page 7: "We get into the habit of living before acquiring the habit of thinking." Page 10: "For everything begins with consciousness and nothing is worth anything except through it." Page 90: "The workman of today works everyday in his life at the same tasks, and this fate is no less absurd. But it is tragic only at the rare moments when it becomes conscious.'"

From the seminars I knew that Dave wasn't liberal, so I went for liberalism. 'Liberalism has nothing to say on meaning, it simply organizes our differences on meaning, i.e. ontology and epistemology, it excuses itself from discussing it. But Camus urges us to pursue it as the most crucial of issues. It has to be. Why wake up every Monday morning?'

'Yeah, but he is still anti-religion.'

'Okay, but what alternative explanations does he have? Anyway, where is it, check this out, Camus talks about the texture of trees, the taste of water and the scent of grass. He says that we describe the world, we classify it, we make up laws about it – we take apart its mechanism. It is then all returned to the atom, and a minuscule invisible planetary system. So science then returns to poetry and art. He says here on page 15: "The soft lines of these hills and the hand of evening on this troubled heart teach me much more. I have returned to my beginning. I realize that if through science I can seize phenomena and enumerate them, I cannot, for all that, apprehend the world." Ultimately, we have competing explanations for the world. Take your pick. Nietzsche even says on page 44: "It is perhaps just dawning on five and six minds that physics too is only an interpretation and arrangement of the world (according to our own requirements, if I may say so!) and not an explanation of the world...".'

'Yeah but Nietzsche is the one who said in Zarathustra...'

'Okay, but this is what I don't get from liberals, on the one hand they quote Nietzsche's critique of religion, and he does criticize religion, but he also severely criticizes liberalism, I mean his critique of public notions of free-will is scathing, page 47: "... a thought comes when 'it' wants, not when 'I' want; so that it is a falsification of the facts to say: the subject 'I' is the condition of the predicate 'think'." Nietzsche says that individual ideas are not arbitrary or autonomous, rather ideas develop from each other – they have an interconnectedness – even if they seem to emerge from nowhere. There is – where does he say it? Here, page 50, "an innate systematism and relationship of concepts".'

'Foucault?'

'That's right.' Taz and the others were looking on, I noticed that they had started to watch the conversation from afar, while pretending to not care, but they were definitely interested. All the points about language and communication that we had discussed on the way down were becoming apparent.

'So you agree with Nietzsche.'

'Not completely, of course not. I'm just saying he can't be taken as totally antagonistic of religion, and there is another way of reading him. But sometimes he's way out, when he talks about the strong on the weak, that's completely out of order. But you know, on the other hand, his will to power stuff is very familiar to mystics cos it is about the nurturing of discipline, the control of the lower self, the desires, and Nietzsche condemns the proliferation of the valorisation of the lower self in his critique of modernity which we as Muslims can agree with, I dunno, but it seems that much of postmodern freedom is the freedom of the lower self, not the freedom of a disciplined soul.'

I thought Dave had grown slightly tired of my preaching, so I decided to relax for a while. We had reached Milton Keynes. I returned to reading Nietzsche (page 115): 'It is more comfortable for our eye to react to a particular object by producing again an image it has often produced before than by retaining what is new and different in an impression: the latter requires more strength, more "morality". To hear something new is hard and painful for the ear; we hear the music of foreigners badly.'

I journeyed to a land of beautiful songbirds – Huhnyms, whose presence in the land was a source of great comfort and joy. Those under the spell of sadness would travel into the forests and lie beneath a tree, waiting for the birds to start singing. Their songs, joyful yet calming, would return the hearer to a state of contentment. They were also gifted with the most attractive feathers, as pleasing to the eye as their songs were to the ear. Servants from the King's palace had sought these feathers, fashioning cushions from them, upon which they relaxed as they would taste its meat. The Huhnyms, though, were difficult to catch; nature had bestowed them with a powerful survival mechanism. As the hunter would approach, the Huhnym would break into song, and the hunter, transfixed, would drop his gun, and shed tears of shame. Hunter after hunter returned to the palace to be executed for non-compliance with the King's command. The King's advisor, not being one of advanced aesthetic sense and seeking the King's pleasure, devised a simple plan that lead to a drastic reduction in the Huhnym population. The hunters would place cotton wool in their ears, making themselves deaf to the Huhnym's petition, and, sure enough, Huhnym after Huhnym was killed and the rooms of the palace became adorned with the feathers of this beautiful bird. The Huhnyms convened a conference, a conference for the birds of beautiful song. They decided to send one of their number to the King's daughter, to persuade her to help. The Princess had been shielded from the song of the Huhnym. The bird flew to the Princess's window and began to sing. The Princess recognized the bird's feathers and realized their plight. Angry, she ran to the cushion factory and burnt it down. The King's men tried to pursue the culprit but all they saw was a trail of tears. The Princess then went to the King and told him what had happened. He listened and then called his advisor. The advisor could not overturn the King's wish to please his daughter. The Huhnyms were called to the palace, and they sang for their survival. The King repented from his greed, if only to please his daughter, and the song of the Huhnyms returned to the forests of this far-off land.

I woke up and looked out again in the hope that Bradford was near. Chesterfield. Good, only about an hour to go. Dave was staring at Saj, who was now sitting in front of us. Saj was listening to the cassette as before, but he was crying. Dave looked at me, and facially enquired as to why he was crying. I shrugged my shoulders. Dave was curious, he leaned forward.

'Ask him?'

I shook my head. Then leaned forward. 'Everything alright?'

'Yeah'.

'The cassette is it?'

'Yeah, he's on about the tree in Madina which would cry when the Prophet moved away from it.'

I knew the section. I had heard it myself, Imam Sulaiman explains through Rumi's poetry the anguish of a tree in Madina which would cry out in pain if the Prophet moved away from it. The Imam breaks down himself while explaining. Dave wanted to know, so I explained it to him, but I don't think he understood. To be honest, I don't think I understood either when I first heard it, but I think it makes more sense as one's faith increases.

Freedom came up again. How does the religious person deal with freedom? Didn't religion mean restriction? Yes, we are not allowed to eat certain foods, but I reminded Dave of the restaurant we had visited on the way out of London. How many kebabs were there? If I was not mistaken he had tried all of them but one? 'Seekh kebab? Shami kebab? Golat kebab? Chapli kebab? Boti kebab? And the mother of all kebabs, Bihari kebab?'

'Donner kebab?'

'No, that's instrumental rationality I'm afraid. We can't eat pork, but it's not like we're not enjoying life. Complete freedom can become impossible. Slight restriction allows for a flowering of colour, spice, variety and choice. Because one is forced to think, to be creative.' We passed the large shopping centre Meadowhall, the green dome reminded me of one of Islam's enduringly beautiful gifts to man, architecture. 'Look at Islamic architecture, we can't draw figures of humans or animals, did that stop us? Of course not. The Dome of the Rock, the Taj Mahal, the Blue Mosque of Istanbul, the Jami Mosque of Isfahan – these are products of freedom and reason, restricted freedom and reason, but are they not amongst the most beautiful buildings known to man? The issue is more complicated. We restrict ourselves in life, but we don't sacrifice beauty and flavour in doing so, it forces us to become more inventive.'

'Look at the Dome of the Rock, it is a product of a type of imagination that employs reason, but it is neither modernist nor postmodernist reason that contributed to that building: it was inspired from elsewhere. It has reason, intricacy, delicacy, subtlety, and pure, sheer, magnificent beauty. Where does it come from? The religious mind is not impoverished, far from it, and to construct a building, it needs to employ some form of rationality.'

Not for the first time today, I ended up giving speeches. It had been a few years since I left the speaker's circuit, and I think I was making up for it today. Dave didn't seem to mind, I felt ashamed that I hadn't spoken to him until today. It had been three years since I first met him, but I only got to know him today. I thought about how I had been talking to the others about isolation, and yet how isolated I was in my own department. I thought they wouldn't be interested, but Dave seemed so. Maybe I was just scared, having to explain everything Muslims have done over the last so many years. It was easier to walk in and walk out.

We dropped him off at home in Leeds and then made our way to Bradford. Tof came up to me, to where Dave was sitting. 'Is he about to convert?'

'I don't think so.'

'But you talked to him for so long?'

'We were just chatting'. It didn't make sense to Toff, either they're enemies or about to convert. Maybe this was the problem. I gave Toff my e-mail address and we arrived back at the mosque at one o'clock in the morning. Everyone walked straight past Osama, ignoring him, which I thought was very polite of them. An hour later, I was in bed, my legs aching, tired but pleased. Another day, another march.

(All references to Camus are from *The Myth of Sisyphus* (New York: Vintage Books, 1955); and all references to Nietzsche are from *Beyond Good and Evil* (London: Penguin Books, 1990)).

4 Making Religion Relevant

Thank you very much for inviting me to speak today. What I hope to do in the next 15 minutes is to ask some questions around the training of imams. For the purposes of this short presentation I will be focusing on imams in Britain.

To begin, the imams that are arriving to serve in British mosques have been trained in the sciences of *'aqida* (the fundamentals of faith), *fiqh* (jurisprudence) and in some cases *tasawwuf* (spirituality). This being the traditional triumvirate of the sciences of religion. The question that we should ask is, does this training in and of itself make the imams fit for purpose for the communities that they serve? As I stated initially, I do not intend to provide many answers in this presentation but I do intend to ask many questions. My approach will be to describe briefly the challenges that face the Muslim community today and then to ask how training prepares imams for these challenges. I will not be discussing the institutions that are cropping up across the country and the associated question that hangs over the infrastructure that we are preparing across the country – are our institutions ready to receive these graduates? I will leave this important aspect of this discussion to one of the later sessions.

The first question to consider is the homogeneity of the British Muslim community. It is immediately obvious that the

British Muslim community is heterogeneous in many different ways: class and ethnicity being two important variables. One immediate example is the difference that is emerging between some Muslim communities in the North and some Muslim communities in the South. To put it simply, an imam arriving in a mosque in Manningham in Bradford will face different challenges to an imam serving the Richmond Muslim Association. As with the North–South discussion in general, this generalisation does not hold across the board as Altrincham Muslim Association in the North or East London Mosque in the South are strong counter-examples.

In my research on Muslim youth cultures in Bradford, I developed a typology of identity types for South Asian Muslim young men. These types are the rude boys, extremists and coconuts. Rude boys mix between three cultures: African-American hip hop, Northern Pakistani and Northern Industrial. The blending of these cultures produces a hybrid identity which is all too familiar in many Northern cities. Extremists are described as such by those who are less practising because they are perceived to have developed an unbalanced approach to the religion. Coconuts are those who are brown on the outside but white on the inside. The terms are pejorative because identity is mutually contested. This typology was developed for South Asian male youth and I'm sure that there will be some crossover for young female Muslims.

To contrast between the coconut and the rude boy, I would suggest that the coconut faces the challenges that are associated with an assimilationist identity within a modern culture. As an individual becomes successful then he or she questions what to take forward and what to leave behind. The questions that seem most common here are those concerning liberalism and science. That is, as an individual begins to achieve within a middle-class cultural context then a part of that cultural integration can include an interrogation of his or her beliefs. I have spoken with many such individuals who have sought advice at this point in their lives. Questions concerning liberalism often relate to the notion of personal freedom, human rights and gender relations. Questions concerning science relate to lay perceptions of materialism and the philosophy of science itself. How does Islam explain our personal experience of freewill? Why are women not equal to men in Islam? Can individualism be a basis for law in Islam? How can religion as a body of knowledge claim to supersede science and its achievements? How many imams are able to answer questions like these today after having received traditional training and how many imams can do so in a way that is intellectually satisfactory and persuasive?

'Within a Western context' – how much should imams know about the intellectual hinterland of the West, Europe and Britain? Do they need to know the difference between empiricism and rationalism? Or the difference between Hume and Kant? Or the origins of the Enlightenment? And its relation to the atheist movement? Do they need to know the history of the social sciences? Or should they be trained in any of the social sciences? Sociology as the sociology of the city or the sociology of modernity? Psychology as child psychology or depth psychology? We would probably need to consider a two-pronged approach here. We should adopt an introductory-level approach to certain subjects such as the sociology of the city, philosophy of science and perhaps child psychology or mental health. Practical knowledge such as recent public policy and the actual names and functions of public institutions may also be important. And we should then adopt a more detailed approach to other subjects such as depth psychology or individualism. 'Individualism' is important because it presents itself to many imams and we need to respond through our own kind of 'individualism'. Individualism is also important because it relates to a theory of prejudice and I would suggest that a centre training imams to act as leaders of the Muslim community should teach 'a theory of prejudice' that will enable imams to deal with the varieties of prejudice that can be placed in their way.

To consider the rude boys, they are the products of inner-city nihilism and as such they experience alienation from many things including meaning and morality. These hollow men are broken by their disconnection from their Lord, their families and their own selves. This feeling of hollowness and total isolation is a most modern and typical circumstance. I have seen young men become transformed from rude boys into the newly-practising and I have felt that the religion that they practise has become a mask which only superficially covers their hollowness. In many senses one feels that they have found religion and yet they have not become religious. The Islam that these young men are being offered is the Islam of outer semblances that replicates so well the cultural commodification that they exhibited as rude boys. The training of imams for this particular group of people will require the development of religious leaders who can replace that hollowness with something more substantial.

Some of us have put together a project called 'Clement's Gate' in Bradford and we are working with Sheikh Saad al-Attas on developing a way of providing guidance to the community that is most relevant. We felt here that the work of Imam Ghazali remains important and relevant to our concerns, especially the *'Ihya' 'Ulum al-Din'* and we have conducted two series of lectures on the books of the *Ihya'*: the first on *'Patience and Gratitude'* and the second on *'The Condemnation of Anger, Rancour and Envy'*. They have been very well-received. A course that trains imams on the *Ihya'* and how to teach it within a Western context may be a useful addition to the curriculum. It could be regarded as a response to the problem of 'hollowness' that I mentioned earlier.

These two examples show that the training that is required for imams has to be specific to the communities that they serve. In the health service we ask for services to be culturally competent for the communities that they serve. So, for example, a diabetes service that offered dietary advice to South Asians without considering the ways in which their diet is different would be regarded as culturally incompetent. In a similar fashion, at present we are asking imams to arrive in communities without knowing their most pressing concerns. A successful lawyer in the city who is finding it difficult to respond to questions on liberalism and the law will require a very different approach to an unemployed youngster who can barely articulate his aspiration and is taking cocaine. Both of them may be distant from their religion, but their experiences of being distant are very different.

Let me move on to the third example and that is of the extremist. The challenge that remains here for imams in Britain – and it is probably one of the greatest challenges to manage – is the potential dual risk of ghettoization and assimilation, which in some towns and cities could happen simultaneously. Extremism is one outcome of this process and it is the result of a total incomprehension about how to integrate into wider society without losing one's integrity. I would suggest here that the role of the imam is crucial. In one sense this is about cultural engagement but in another sense it is also about political engagement because the political question is one question that we will always have to answer because of what 'Muslimness' itself can do to rupture Western self-confidence and because of the socio-economic conditions of a large part of our community. This political engagement requires knowledge of British political history at national and local level and in terms of sentiment and party politics. For example, in order to provide some leadership to a community in a city run by the Tories and the Liberal Democrats, it is important to know the difference between being a Liberal and being a libertarian. And if ghettoization is a communal defence mechanism, then the question will be how to lead the community out of ghettoization without risking assimilation later on.

But this is also about cultural integration and I found this to be one of the most important ways of sedimenting Muslim identity within a Western experience. That is, those who are familiar in one way or another with poetry or literature such as Wordsworth or Dickens seem to me to be better able to understand the nuances and subtleties of polite conversation that lies at the heart of British character. I would call here for some form of religious leadership in this area that will help to generate a language of integration that we need so much.

On its website, the Cambridge Muslim College has the following aphorism: 'Four things support the world: the learning of the wise, the justice of the great, the prayers of the good, and the valour of the brave.' This aphorism describes the functions of the ideal imam as I would see him: as the saint (*wali*) – the prayers of the good; the jurist (*faqih*) – the learning of the wise; and the leader (*amir*) – the justice of the great and the valour of the brave. Whether this is practically achievable is dependent more on the personalities themselves than any training programme. I leave this question for you to consider but it would be an ideal situation if each of our great cities had several imams who combined these characteristics within their expansive souls.

There are other types that I could have mentioned. I can think here of converts, asylum seekers, children from dual-heritage couples, and the newly-practising (as I call them). I hope that the examples that I have mentioned have made the case for a form of training that is robust yet relevant.

Before I conclude, I would like to highlight one more point about the training of imams and concerning their role as advisors on parenting and family life. This is a very dynamic area at present and there seems to be much crossover with the previous issues of identity. We have a developing discourse around gender which is impacting on society as a whole while young Muslims are integrating authentic (or what are presented as authentic) religious teachings on family life within their cultural norms – South Asian and British. Many are managing this successfully but I hope that I am not exaggerating when I suggest that many are also finding this very difficult. The imam seems to be the first port of call and he has to respond to families in crisis by providing the right answers at the right moments. Training that covers family dynamics would be very useful here. I would not wish to suggest a model to be incorporated into the programme but the contribution of what depth psychology could offer here may be worthwhile investigating. For example, abusive husbands repeat the patterns of abuse that they may have experienced at home from their fathers. Husbands may find it very difficult to engage emotionally with their families because of a lack of emotional development in their own childhood. Wives may project blame on to their husbands for experiences that they may have had previously in their lives. Imams are often faced with these situations and many offer advice without any previous training in family psychology. It may be worth considering whether an imam should refer on cases in these situations. Should the imam act as a family counsellor in these situations or should he pass on the couple to a family counsellor? This needs serious consideration and applies equally to other areas of concern such as mental health and substance misuse.

How we train imams will depend upon the priority that is given to the various functions that I have described above and the role that we would expect of our imams in delivering these functions either as signposts or as the persons charged with the responsibility of service itself. In summary, I would suggest that the traditional teaching methods in 'aqida and fiqh specifically are as important as the foundational necessities of Islamic learning, however, as the examples that I have mentioned have shown, there are many aspects to the Western cultural experience which will require further training on the specificities of the communities that these imams will serve in order to make them the best that they can be.

5 Seven Faces of Freedom

Dear ladies and gentlemen, I wish to begin by thanking you for inviting me to speak today at the fiftieth anniversary of the Anglo-Liberal Fellowship of the South. It is an honour to speak to you today and it is probably indicative of the relevance of this topic to current political debate that you have asked me to speak to you today on Islam, freedom and liberalism.

What I intend to do as suggested by my title '*Seven Faces of Freedom*' is to work thorough seven ways in which a Muslim might respond to this question of Islam and freedom. I will work through each response or interaction if you like. The suggestion at the outset might very well be that Islam and freedom or Islam and liberalism are diametrically opposed. I would hope that by the end of this lecture I have managed to persuade you that this relation is more complicated and perhaps less oppositional than is commonly supposed.

So let me begin with the first face of freedom. The first face of freedom is the feeling of freedom itself – the phenomenology of freedom, the experience of being free. British society may suggest that religion restricts the ability of individuals to experience this. I can think here of Bertrand Russell's and Friedrich Nietzsche's view on freedom. Russell saw religion as a series of moral codes that restricted the ability of the individual to enjoy fully the possibilities and pleasures of life. Nietzsche instead saw the possibility of freedom and the feeling of freedom as emerging from the will to power. Adopting a sociological perspective, one could say that freedom in today's society is experienced through the reading of a great novel – to enjoy the heights of cultural expression that fire our imagination towards new destinations – or that freedom could be the feeling experienced as one rides a horse across a beach while on holiday. Freedom could also be the experience of the chief executive of a large financial company who decides to launch a takeover of a rival company. These are all forms of freedom that can be experienced and it is not immediately obvious that there is a contradiction per se between what Islam would advocate and all of these expressions or feelings.

But the face of freedom that I wish to focus on here is the feeling of freedom as flight – as a lightness of being – and I would like to suggest that religion and Islam in its more mystical or spiritual manifestations encourages a lightness of being – a feeling of freedom – but a spiritual lightness of being. As the Sufi poet says:

> In my spirit I am like the heavens;
> Bodily I am mere speck of dust.[1]

It is this being on the earth but distanced from it: this asceticism that lifts one above and out of the material towards an experience of freedom – from the lower, desirous self towards the Eternal and the Divine – which Islam makes possible. It is a feeling, an experience of freedom, as exemplified by the whirling dervishes of Rumi's spiritual order but it is unlike other feelings. It is neither a celebration of sensual pleasure nor does it involve the exercise of power. It is a spiritual lightness of being which is experienced as freedom from all except the One. So I would like to begin by saying that this form of freedom is possible and indeed desirable.

The second face of freedom is creativity and originality. The argument here suggests that religion restricts the freedom of creative and artistic people. The first question to ask at this point is whether there is such a thing as Islamic art? Does Islam as a religion allow for art, for creative expression? The answer is that of course it does. There are norms and values concerning this art but it does exist all over the world. One only has to think of the mosque in Madina in Saudi Arabia, the Alhambra in Grenada in Spain, Iznik tiles in Turkey, Moroccan interiors, Pakistani qawwalis, Damascene chants, Ottoman calligraphy, the Taj Mahal, and Isfahani mosques and carpets to know that Islamic art does indeed exist. The second question that one could ask is whether this art is of any value? Does it add to creativity and to beauty? This may be a matter of personal choice and taste but there are a sizeable group of people who would hold that Islamic art does contribute to the beauty of the world. And all of this beauty is derived from the freedom of the artist as he has stared at a piece of paper and then attempted to translate what was within his imagination into a material form. Islam here has not restricted the freedom of creativity, instead, it has encouraged it and the world is more beautiful because of it.

A related point here is that the originality of spirit that lead to modernity was somehow rejected by Islamic nations. This may be the case but as authors such as Hasan le Gai Eaton have pointed out, this may have been for good reasons.[2] The worst wars in history were experienced on European soil. Poem after poem documented the deep despair that these wars brought upon the human condition. By refusing modernity, or perhaps the extremes of the caustic mixture of industrialisation and capitalism, Islamic nations protected themselves from some of the worst that humanity has ever witnessed.

And there is another point to be made here about originality. The purpose of the religion in Islam is to return man to the Origin – being original, constantly refreshing oneself or one's views, is not as important as being connected to the Origin of all through which all creativity can then be expressed.[3] This is the freedom of the religious imagination and it is this freedom that has given us Islamic art – a sign of the Beauty that lies beyond.

Now let us move on to the third face of freedom and this relates to reason and rationality. There is a common thread that runs through public debate. It goes something like this: the Enlightenment taught humanity to think for itself by championing rationality. Our society is the beneficiary of such an intellectual hinterland and as such we are all free to think as we please. This is what distinguishes us from others, less modern and less civilised than ourselves. The assumption is that everyone is a rational being. Instead, I would wish to suggest that rationality cannot be assumed, and that it remains a possibility for most.

As the influence of religion has declined, the social sciences have taken up the mantle of explaining and prescribing for human thought and behaviour. Consequently, the social sciences have developed from their earlier theorising through experimentation and discipline expansion towards what they have become today: a great monolith of academic application and study from anthropology through sociology to psychology and all that lies in-between and across.[4]

Can a century's worth or more of the social sciences add anything to the lay understanding of rationality as described above. Let us return to the basic postulate: 'I am free to think' (this has implications for freedom as freedom understood today is dependent upon rationality). I would suggest that there are three ways at least in which such an understanding of rationality is circumscribed.

First of all, let us consider psychoanalysis. It may have been the case that Freud was incorrect in certain aspects of his theory – but his suggestion of the interplay between the id, ego and superego through defence mechanisms and the role of the unconscious in general are profound limitations on rationality. Rationality here can be rationalisation – what one person considers a free thought may in fact be a consequence of some tension between his id, ego and superego. The role of the emotions, their origins and the unconscious all exert some influence upon our freedom 'to think independently'.

Secondly, as studies in the psychology of reasoning have found, common forms of reasoning in everyday life are flawed. By way of example judgements under uncertainty consider heuristics –

shorthand for logic – as a form of psychological reasoning. In the heuristic of availability, people reason according to the information that is available to them such that in the case of risk, for example, risks such as travelling by airplane cause more fear and anxiety than walking near a river although more people have drowned in the latter. However, because there is more information widely available on the risks associated with air travel then there is a greater fear associated with this risk.

Thirdly, the sociology of knowledge which continues on from the psychology of reasoning considers the structure of meaning that is available to many people, its context within the intellectual landscape and its relevance. Essentially, terms have meaning within their cultural histories – 'progress' means something within the context of modernity or 'identity' means something within the context of postmodernity. As such, key terms that become part of everyday language and through which we make sense of our lives and relations to each other are heavily laden with the weight that is the history of culture. Our reasoning is therefore heavily circumscribed by the languages that are available to us and if the standard of education is poor, then the capacity for personal freedom is further limited.

For all these three reasons, everyday rationality is limited. This does not mean that it is not possible. Rationality can become possible if one is trained to understand one's own psychology, understand the different forms of logic and reasoning and understand etymology and cultural history. If one can succeed in learning these three kinds of knowledge and skill, then one can begin to walk the path to freedom.

I would like to move on now to the fourth face of freedom and this is as individualism in law. What does Islam have to say about individualism in law? What is the Islamic approach to human rights? I would like to consider this issue from two perspectives: the first as whether appealing to human rights makes any sense within the Islamic tradition and secondly to what extent is Islamic law itself compatible with liberal individualism?

With regards to the question of whether Muslims have any difficulty in appealing to human rights, well, I think the experience of the war on terror has been one in which Muslims have consistently and repeatedly called for the protection of the human rights of individuals whether this be from kidnapping, torture or imprisonment. This appeal to freedom, to liberty, as an individual from the state or the law has been used in Western and Eastern countries.

The more difficult scenario is the compatibility or otherwise of liberal individualism with Islamic law. It is certainly the case that certain foundational aspects of Islamic law, for example, the objectives of the Sharia, are quite clearly compatible with individualism – these objectives are the protection of life, honour, mind, property and faith in relation to the individual. Classical Islamic scholars such as al-Shatibi put forward these objectives as a way of explaining the purposes of the Sharia itself. There is obviously some overlap here. But there are three areas of difference: the extent and manner of punishment, the recognition of categories beyond the individual and a disagreement on what in some cases constitutes the good. All of these are examples of areas in which Islam is felt to restrict freedom.

These discussions of the faces of freedom have so far focused upon the abstract, and I would like to now move on to look at three faces of freedom which are embedded in cultural realities. That is, we should note some familiarity towards them. The fifth face of freedom that I wish to mention is Muslim identity politics. This is an expression of freedom, a yearning perhaps, but one that is rejected by its intended audience. Muslim identity politics takes after the other forms of identity politics that we have become so used to: the black civil rights movement, feminism etc. But in this particular case the advocates of Muslim identity politics are calling for their recognition as Muslims, to be free and equal as Muslims. However, this is not just about equality, it is about the freedom to be different – about the right to stand apart from others, the crowd, as one wishes and assert a form of distinctiveness which challenges stigma and discrimination. It is certainly a way of being free; it is a call to freedom but one that disrupts the social and discursive convention of its environs. Much of what we have experienced in British Islam over the last two decades can be put down to Muslim identity politics: the emergence of Muslim youth groups during the eighties, the formation of the Muslim Council of Britain in the nineties, the campaigns for the inclusion of religion in the 2001 census, the campaigns against Salman Rushdie's *The Satanic Verses* – these are all expressions of Muslim identity politics.

The campaign against *The Satanic Verses* is perhaps the most relevant here. It represented a total disconnect as the two opposing groups could not understand each other's positions at all: one asserting the absolute importance of free speech and the other calling for respect for the sacred. The identity politics paradigm would have suggested here that this campaign was similar to the civil rights campaign against the Black and White Minstrels and golliwogs, that it was an attempt to challenge the culture of misrepresentation that devalued their identity and hence restricted their freedom. Again, this is a form of freedom that has been readily and even enthusiastically adopted by Muslims.

The sixth face of freedom is liberalism as humanism – again this is embedded in cultural practice. This form of liberalism is the liberalism of the literate culture, of scholars, poets and intellectuals, of love, kindness and thoughtfulness. This is the genteel liberalism of humanistic culture. It is not unknown to Muslims, either historically or culturally. The Andalusia of Ibn 'Arabi, the poetry of Rumi and its collective manifestations, the gentle urbanity of the Sufis from Delhi or Damascus and the aphorisms of the great North African sage Abu Madyan are all examples of humanism and humanist cultures. George Makdisi – the American historian of ideas – has written of the translation of humanism itself from Arab to European culture in the period leading up to the Renaissance. This history or collective memory is being explored at present in the British Muslim experience though unfortunately there is some attempt to meet postmodern bourgeois cultural nihilism at some median point – alas! A new world of letters – of poetry and art – that reaches deep within the Muslim soul to re-emerge and proclaim is present but still nascent. It is nascent because the present Muslim religious experience is shallow, but as the collective Muslim soul delves deeper into its own cultural archive to discover and then appreciate a humanism of its own, then it will begin to discover a long lost friend – and like Rumi after Shams Tabrizi – then manifest this obvious beauty within itself and then to others. This is a form – an expression – of freedom as well but one that remains in the main a potential for the Muslim soul.

The final face of freedom that I wish to mention is liberalism as nihilism. This is the freedom of the lower soul – a hedonism that chases the crass materialism that surrounds us. This nihilism means different things to different classes – to most Muslims in Britain that come from more deprived areas, this nihilism is a form of showmanship – a brazen advertisement of self as achiever whether this is in the form of glistening metallic paint or designer clothes wear. This is a form of freedom as well. It is a form of freedom taken on by those who have been denied other freedoms by circumstance and experience. Family breakdown, poor education or a lack of job prospects mean that for some their options in life are severely limited. And so they taste the freedom that is available to them within an inner-city environment – the freedom to escape to anywhere else without actually escaping. This is a form of nihilism – an abdication – a running away because there is nothing to stay for, it is the pursuit of pleasure, of sensuality through which one can pretend that life may one day get better when one knows that by continuing like this, it will only get worse. There is no freedom of mind here, no flight of spirit, no rising ambition, just a consumption of imagery and produce to while away the time. Hollow men, stuffed men? Leaning together, headpiece filled with straw? Shade without motion? These are not soldiers in the trenches of the First World War but young men lost in the inner cities of our postmodern era. The driving round in flash unaffordable cars, standing around on street corners, gang fights, evening after evening spent with the highs of cheap drugs, this is the liberalism as nihilism offered up through capitalist, consumerist culture to those who can know no other freedom. It has been accepted by the thousands – as if they had some choice, it comes naturally to them, most would say that they enjoy it and it is the seventh face of freedom.

And so we have our seven freedoms: freedom as phenomenology, freedom as creativity, freedom as rationality, freedom as individualism in law, freedom as Muslim identity politics, freedom as humanism and freedom as nihilism. It has been my intention to suggest that Islam is not inherently against freedom as such, and also to show that Muslim cultures have different normative ways to express their freedom. I would also hope to suggest that though religion and Islam itself are considered to be restricting influences on freedom – disciplinary mechanisms perhaps – nevertheless, there remain numerous ways in which Islam and Muslims interact with freedom and that a liberal Muslim culture is certainly possible in the abstract and in reality.

6 Muslims and the Social[1]

It was Margaret Thatcher who famously commented on the central role of individualism in government that 'there is no such thing as society' at a time of triumphant economic individualism and ascending cultural individualism.[2] The election of New Labour heralded a change in this policy, in Tony Blair's words: 'A new dawn has come, has it not?' Was this new dawn the return of the social to government policy? Academics such as Robert Putnam, Richard Sennett and Anthony Giddens have advised on how to return the social to society and 10 years of New Labour have witnessed a massive increase in the size of the welfare state in some areas and a streamlining of service provision in other areas. It is David Cameron now who criticises Thatcher and this development through his position: 'There is such a thing as a society, it is just not the same as the state.'[3] That is, that there is a place for the social in public life, whether as part of the state or aligned with it. Family tax credits, child benefits, neighbourhood renewal, regeneration, health action zones, education action zones, volunteering and third sector commissioning are all examples of current British policy areas that involve the incorporation of the social into state-funded activities – that is the state through its financial support makes some link (other than through direct service delivery) with the way society is structured informally away from the state.[4]

Where are Muslims in relation to the social? And after 10 years of New Labour, how have Muslims been incorporated into the formulation and then delivery of programmes that have required some wider networking? In this chapter I will review some books that have all been published in the last few years that examine this issue but from different perspectives. The discussion as framed above is an abstracted account of the situation as it is; but the situation as it is does not express itself in abstract terms – that is, the social does not exist as the social, instead it exists as the cultural and the religious. And this is the central cause of the problem in this British debate: the government recognises the importance of the social in the alleviation of societal problems and yet it faces having to deal with an expression of the social that challenges its self-image – or at least is interpreted as a challenge to the self-image of the state as a neutral arbiter and fair provider.[5]

The tension between the individual and the social was played out in the Stephen Lawrence enquiry into the murder of a young black London teenager. Previous race relations legislation had focused on racism as a problem of individual discrimination. The Stephen Lawrence enquiry, which was chaired by a senior Judge, William MacPherson, and included John Sentamu (who later became the Archbishop of York) and Richard Stone (from the Runnymede Trust's Islamophobia Commission) as advisors, concluded that the problem of racism in society was an institutional problem and therefore the enquiry advised the British government to consider tackling racism as a structural – a social – problem.[6] This was accepted by the government and was brought into law in 2000 as the Race Relations Amendment Act. This required amongst other things all public sector organisations to advance race equality through recognising the social dimensions of prejudice. Prejudice was located at this moment not in the individual where it may be expressed, but in the social.

This understanding was to face a challenge in the summer of 2001 when Bradford, Burnley and Oldham experienced major rioting. The threat of the far right had brought many youth on to the streets who then later went on to clash with the police. In one sense, this rioting could have been interpreted as an expression of frustration against structural racism and inequality, but instead the publishing of the Ouseley Report in the immediate aftermath of the riots framed the national response through its articulation of the self-segregation narrative.[7] This suggested that the problem was with the community itself: the inequalities that the Muslim community experienced were not due to structural racism, but instead to a refusal to integrate into wider society. The Muslim community – this narrative suggested – was seeking to isolate itself through a form of moral protectionism and this was leading to communities in Northern cities (which had large Muslim populations) living 'parallel lives'. The government asked Ted Cantle, the former chief executive of Nottingham City Council, amongst others, to lead an enquiry into the causes of the riots and the final report identified the lack of community cohesion as the cause of the problem.[8] The Home Office at this point set up a Community Cohesion Unit and local councils up and down the country were encouraged to set up community cohesion initiatives. These ranged from truancy reduction to linking schools. The shift in emphasis from MacPherson to Cantle was important and had a profound impact on the progress of the race agenda under New Labour.

To borrow an overused phrase, the elephant in the room during this period was and remains Muslim identity politics. It has caused a rupture in conventional political wisdom and remains an enigma to public policy. It is important to recognise the provenance of Muslim identity politics that emerged during the eighties as a form of public campaigning as Muslims began to ask that they be considered as Muslims and not as Asians or blacks. This was politically significant and had consequences for the types of services, such as Muslim schools for example, to be delivered to large ethnic minority populations that were Muslim. Though the Race Relations Amendment Act of 2000, which was a positive step forward, did not recognise Muslims, community cohesion as policy did recognise Muslims but as the source of ghettoization and self-segregation.

Identity, Ethnic Diversity and Community Cohesion is a collection of papers presented to a seminar jointly organised by the ESRC Identities and Social Action Programme and the Runnymede Trust in September 2005. Part One of this book contains contributions from policy officers and the book begins with a chapter by Henry Tam, one of the key architects of Labour's policy on civil renewal, in which he examines the fragmentation of civil society and its possible causes including moral decline, a loss of patriotism, social mobility, insecure identities and the unequal distribution of power. The prescription for this problem is building progressive solidarity. In his description of progressive solidarity, Tam refers to the central tension of the incorporation of Muslim subjectivity into the pursuit of the social. He distinguishes progressive solidarity from rigid solidarity which is 'formed out of imposed compliance to a fixed set of social arrangements wherein people have to fulfil their assigned functions and accept their lot in life'.[9] He continues, 'The challenge is how to open up the channel for individual development while enabling people to retain and cultivate a rich sense of solidarity.'[10] Tam, as a leading New Labour theoretician and practitioner of the social, indicates here the dilemma that a Labour administration had with extending the social to include Muslim subjectivity. It was community cohesion as policy which provided one important answer to this question, at least from 2002–2007. It suggested that 'the Muslim social' was not a positive value, but rather an exaggeration, to such an extent that it had become a problem. Muslims were too social, or perhaps too social amongst themselves – what Robert Putnam would describe as 'bonding social capital'. This was the popularised version of community cohesion.

Nick Johnson, one of the policy officers who has worked closely with Cantle over the years, provides the next chapter which clarifies the Commission for Racial Equality's position on this issue. This is strategically important because it was Trevor Phillips' intervention in the months after the 7th July bombings of 2005 that helped locate the integration debate within the much greater terrorism debate (that is, that Muslims are more likely to become terrorists because they come from communities that lead parallel lives). He took Cantle's main thesis of parallel lives and suggested that Britain was 'sleepwalking into segregation'.[11] Coincidentally, the speech by Phillips was delivered at the same time as this seminar was held. Johnson, instead, identifies the three strands to the CRE's interpretation of community cohesion: equality, participation and interaction. Equality through formal, public institutions, participation with formal, public institutions and interaction with wider society. Integration, according to Johnson, can only be achieved through all three – this contrasts rather sharply with Trevor Phillips' contemporaneous speech.

Part Two consists of four empirical chapters that examine some of the assumptions around this policy area. Rogaly and Taylor look at the reliance of the New Deal for Communities on the notion of a community in relation to three estates in Norwich. They find that the community is in transition with members constantly leaving and joining. This notion of a local community requires some myth-making and new members express their adherence to the community through their commitment to the myth. Clarke and others in 'Home, Identity and Community Cohesion' describe this myth-making as the construction of a 'golden age' discourse. They refer to the declining influence of British identity and yet their interviewees had strong local identities as Plymouthians or Bristolians, contrasting their local attachments which made sense and had some form of anchored meaning with the vague and evasive notion of Britishness. Hewstone, a social psychologist who specialises in social contact theory, and others provide the final paper which looks at the nature of contact between different groups of people and the effect that this can have on their view of others i.e. the relation between contact and prejudice. Hewstone argues that if social capital can be positive or negative then the challenge for society is to encourage as many positive contacts as possible. Hewstone examines the effects of larger or smaller numbers of outgroup contacts and the nature of contact itself: direct or indirect (associates having direct contacts). Hewstone notes that if the numbers of outgroup contacts are not large then direct or indirect contact can have positive effects on intergroup relations.

The final part of this book is a collection of four reflective pieces by academics in this area of study. Each adds to the previous discussions through their observations. Alexander notes the emphasis in Johnson's piece that segregation arises as a matter of cultural choice which leads to separation and the perpetuation of oppositional values and the emphasis is therefore on culture rather than structure as the primary driver of exclusion and alienation. Similarly, Gavron notes that the emphasis on bridging capital could be detrimental to bonding capital (upon which it is dependent) and she states that any initiatives that jeopardise mutual support systems within ethnic minority communities in favour of more generic support mechanisms may lead to harm as well as good. Parekh notes the various usages of the term multiculturalism and calls for clarity of definition in its use and he prefers a multiculturalism that is an interactive cultural diversity within a single but internally plural composite culture. Finally, Brah refers to the various factors that help constitute identity including economic, representational and the personal. Muslim subjectivity, therefore, is multi-faceted.

As mentioned earlier, and indicated in several of the chapters in this book, multiculturalism as public policy has come under sustained attack after the 2001 riots and the 7th July bombings. 'Multiculturalism has failed' is a common assertion today. One of the supporters of multiculturalism as policy is Tariq Modood, professor in sociology at Bristol University. His book *Multiculturalism* published in 2007 can be read as a defence of this policy at a time when the general drift was in the opposite direction. It is an accessible, clear, methodical and persuasive defence of multiculturalism. Modood begins with an examination of Will Kymlicka's contribution to the debate. Kymlicka is one the leading political theorists in this area and his approach is to argue for an inclusive political theory from a liberal perspective. For example, Kymlicka criticises Rawl's depiction of the liberal state as being culture-neutral and Kymlicka suggests that this is not possible. Instead the state actively promotes certain cultural identities and in doing so it discriminates against other cultural identities. Modood suggests here that Kymlicka is exerting a liberal bias because if the state is culturally biased then surely it must be religiously biased as well? Instead, Modood argues for an evolutionary secularism that is pragmatic in its approach to cultural diversity. Different groups will have different demands and the state can therefore respond in kind such that a variable geometry of multicultural accommodation emerges. In order to do this, Modood suggests that there needs to be some recognition of the social as expressed by minority groups but that this recognition needs to be wary of reifying or idealising such notions of cultural or religious public expression. This can be achieved through recognising a form of citizenship that is pluralist, multilogical and dispersed. By this he means that a citizen could be British as well as a Southerner, this plurality of self-expression is in constant dialogue, and that the sites of expression and exchange are numerous – that is, it is not only the state that works on this.

If Modood's study has a policy context then Anne Phillips' *Multiculturalism without Culture* also has a political context and this is the debate between feminism and multiculturalism. If multiculturalism is about the expansion of political norms to embrace cultural diversity, then one of the checks on such an expansion is the effects that this could have on the rights of women from ethnic minority communities. Or, if the social is to be expanded to include the cultural and the religious, then one of the checks on this is the rights of women. This debate has been one of the backcloth discussions to the multiculturalism debate as a whole but it was propelled to the discursive frontline by Susan Okin in her article 'Is multiculturalism bad for women?'[12] This article stated in clear terms that recognising cultural diversity was severely problematic for feminists as there were many issues which, if accommodated, could mean harming the rights of ethnic minority women. Anne Phillips is one of the leading feminist scholars in the West, and, as such, has been involved in these debates for many years. She refers to this debate and has a natural affinity with the position that is concerned about the dangers posed by embracing cultural diversity. However, she also begins her book by mentioning her discomfort with the way in which pro-feminist arguments have been used to justify racism and the pursuit of military objectives in Afghanistan. This has made her reflect upon Okin's position statement and in one sense her book can be read as a lengthy response to Okin. It could also be read as an attempt to approach the same issues that Modood raises concerning multiculturalism but from a feminist perspective. If Modood's argument can be read as a case for moderate secularism that eschews foundations and theories for pragmatism and negotiation, then a question to consider while reading Phillip's book is whether this approach is possible in the case of women's rights?

Phillips states at the outset that she is arguing for a different kind of multiculturalism – but for multiculturalism nonetheless. She picks up in one sense where Modood ends by stating at the beginning of her book:

> I maintain that those writing on multiculturalism (supporters as well as critics) have exaggerated not only the unity and solidity of cultures but the intractability of value conflict as well, and often misrecognised highly contextual political dilemmas as if these reflected deep value disagreement.[13]

Phillips spends a considerable amount of time problematizing conceptions of culture and warns against essentialist readings of culture while refusing to deny that people are cultural beings. Such that for example in the case of forced marriage, culture may explain forced marriages amongst South Asians, however, most parents are not violent in trying to force their choices upon their own children. She questions the stereotypes employed in 'cultural defence' arguments made in law: women are viewed as quiet victims and men as aggressively violent. The issue here is the explanatory role of culture – that the men are violent because of their culture. Phillips disallows this form of defence and believes it should not be tolerated. She states that this position misrepresents individuals from different religions and cultures as less than autonomous agents and furthermore the blame is attributed to an entire culture rather than to individual aberration.

Similarly, making blanket assertions about the abuse of culture can conceal the complexity of choices that are played out in everyday lives. Such that the hijab ban in French schools in 2004 may legally protect some who have been forced to wear the hijab but may oppress those who choose to wear the hijab. Similarly, with forced marriages, legislating against culture as a whole does not recognise the complexity of the choices that underlie the practice of arranged marriage. This is similar to 'the pathologisation of culture' trend that was experienced in the community cohesion debate. It reflects the tension that exists when the social is extended to include the cultural and the religious. Phillips goes further by stating that the pathologisation of culture or religion to encourage exit amongst group members can actually discourage internally generated change and that this can be problematic for those who are oppressed but who nevertheless retain a strong, normative commitment to their group. Phillips' is a defence of multiculturalism which is grounded in the rights of the individual but one which recognises that culture and religion can form an important part of an individual's self-identity.

Gray has written on the two forms of liberalism: Enlightenment rationalism versus a *modus vivendi* approach which Modood translates as a hardened and a moderate form of secularism when applied to public policy.[14] Labour when turning its attention towards the social adopted a *modus vivendi* or moderate approach to public policy but this has been challenged by an Enlightenment-rationalist approach when the state considers what the social actually means for Muslim communities. Modood has laid out a political approach that checks against this development when considering Muslim communities and Phillips considers the issues raised specifically around the rights of women and constantly refers back to a *modus vivendi* approach as a surer way of recognising the problem and then resolving it.

If there is a problem in her approach, then it is her reluctance to agree to allow cultural groups regulatory authority over the members of their group. The problem here for the state is that this is already in place. Marriages and other forms of social activity are already informally regulated by strong cultures that are thriving in many European cities. The problem for the liberal theorist here is fivefold. First of all, many individuals have freely agreed to live their lives according to these norms. Secondly, and contrary to the first point, many individuals do not have a choice but to adhere to the religious norms of their groups and exit is not an option for them (for example, in relation to marriage). Thirdly, this unregulated sector is not free from abuse, and because it is the realm of culture, the abuse can perversely be allowed to continue because public sector officials may refuse to involve themselves in some cases for fear of being accused of racism. Fourthly, where the service provision may require choices on the part of the consumer, then the provision of an appropriate service is a matter of choice by way of equal citizenship even if this includes the recognition of cultural or religious identity. Fifthly, though the state does not recognise these points at present, it nevertheless has to respond to them when in the form of the police or the health services it has to deal with an unregulated cultural issue that requires the intervention of the state. Phillips' solution here does not answer any of these problems.

The recognition of cultural diversity is not just about the law or politics, it is also about the welfare state and though citizens of the state share the law and welfare state, it is the redistribution of resources through the welfare state that asks burning questions of our mutuality. This question was asked by David Goodhart in 2004 when he wrote his now famous article-as-political-intervention 'Too diverse?' which suggested that increasing diversity would challenge the togetherness that is necessary for the continuation of the welfare state.[15] This issue is explored in detail in a book of collected papers edited by Keith Banting and Will Kymlicka on 'Multiculturalism and the welfare state'. In their introduction, Banting and Kymlicka highlight three ways in which multicultural policies could be regarded as eroding the welfare state. They name these the crowding out effect, the corroding effect and the misdiagnosis effect. They present the case for each and then provide some counterpoints. The crowding out effect refers to the notion that campaigning for multicultural recognition detracts and takes away from campaigns for socio-economic redistribution. The counter-claim is that campaigns for multicultural recognition continue to keep the pursuit of justice in the political arena and there remains little evidence that people who were campaigning on multicultural policies have been distracted or averted away from campaigning on socio-economic issues. The corroding effect suggests that campaigning on multicultural issues erodes trust and solidarity between citizens who share the same welfare state by emphasising the differences between them. The counter-claim states that this position assumes that there was inter-ethnic trust and solidarity beforehand whereas multicultural policies are usually brought into place where ethnic minority communities have experienced longstanding exclusion. The misdiagnosis effect suggests that campaigners for multiculturalism misdiagnose the problem as being due to culture rather than race or class. The counter-claim is that multiculturalism does not have a primary foundational claim that cultural inequalities have primacy over other forms of inequalities. Instead, multicultural theorists would suggest that cultural inequalities play a role in inequality as a whole and that this interacts with other factors such as class.

The first part of this book examines the central thesis of whether increasing support for multicultural policies damages support for the welfare state. The second part of the book contains a country-by-country analysis of the same issue and the final part of the book contains some theoretical reflections on the data. Banting et al. critically examine the evidence against two forms of this argument: the heterogeneity/redistribution debate and the recognition/redistribution debate. The first suggests that heterogeneity itself can damage social cohesion whereas the second states that multicultural policies damage social cohesion.

Banting and others investigate the possibility of this across several industrialised nations and find that there is no evidence to suggest that this is occurring 'There is no systematic pattern of countries that have adopted strong multicultural policies seeing erosion in their welfare states relative to countries that have resisted such programmes.'[16] They did find some evidence to support the heterogeneity/redistribution trade-off but this was related to the speed with which immigrant populations were increasing. That is, there seems to be a decrease in social spending in areas of rapidly increasing immigrant populations but this seems to be mitigated through the use of multicultural policies, the authors argue that this may be because the policies require an acknowledgement of diversity.

There are several case studies in this book and these include examinations of these issues in North America, Britain, the Netherlands and Germany. Hero and Preus found that there was no correlation between the uptake of multicultural policies and the size of the welfare state in various US states and using surveys such as the British Social Attitudes Survey Evans found that it was difficult to substantiate the claim that there is a trade-off between the uptake of multiculturalist policies and the welfare state in Britain.[17] The Netherlands which had a strong multiculturalist policy has moved to weaken the policies but the argument for this was that multiculturalist policies were causing further division so they had to be discarded in order to unite the population. Kraus and Schonwalder writing on Germany state that multiculturalist policies may not progress because the state does not regard its immigrants as long-term residents, does not wish to encourage ethnic solidarities, and that stronger ethnic solidarities are seen as a danger to the cohesiveness of the state as a whole.[18] These examples show how the debate is playing out across several countries. Certainly, the debate has not concluded, and the evidence from those countries that have had inclusive policies over an extended period of time is that there is no clear trade-off between the incorporation of multiculturalist policies and a continuing commitment to the welfare state.

The final part of the book contains a couple of theoretical reflections on the findings reported in the book. Miller examines the evidence presented in the book and contrasts it against the criticisms of those that suggest that multicultural policies damage the cohesion of the state.[19] He agrees with the critics that a redistributive state is dependent upon a certain level of cohesion and that this is challenged by a certain form of multiculturalism – he terms this multiculturalism as ideology as against multiculturalism as policy. Multiculturalism as ideology encourages the ethnic group to develop an identity that challenges the wider national consensus and he suggests that if there is a solution then it is in the form of a 'multiculturalism that extends special treatment to cultural minorities when, but only when, this serves to integrate them more closely into the wider community as equal citizens.'[20] In practice, this means that extending opportunities for minorities in one context may in another context lead to increasing polarisation. In the final chapter, Myles and St-Arnaud suggest that successful inclusion will require economic and political incorporation but they concur with Miller that ultimately the answer to this question will depend upon the particular policies adopted and their effect upon support for the welfare state.[21] If there is a gap in the analysis this book offers, it is in the lack of examination of the kinds of multicultural policies that are being debated. There is a great variety in the type of multicultural policy and the variance is dependent upon the sector and the extent of intervention. A discussion on this variety and its effect on support for the welfare state would have been useful.

There is an air of urgency around this debate and sometimes this is attributed to the terrorism connection. However, the demographic projections for many British cities including Birmingham and Leicester and for many parts of London such as Brent, Tower Hamlets and Newham suggest that this issue will become more pressing as ethnic minority populations begin to form ethnic majorities. As these ethnic minorities have strong cultures at present then it will be important for the state and local government to be clear-headed about how to respond to these challenges. The debate in this area over the last 10 years has shown that the debate itself is not straightforward. As Labour, encouraged by Putnam, Sennett and Giddens, has considered incorporating the social, so it has faced challenges from Cantle, Goodhart and Trevor Phillips when including the social has meant incorporating the cultural or the religious. Modood, through his intervention, has offered a way to think through this and the books by Anne Phillips and Banting et al. provide a thorough analysis of how this issue can be transcended when considering women's rights and the welfare state respectively. In many respects, the outcome of the debate is dependent upon the type of immigrant and the kind of policy. Immigrants who are regarded as free-riders or policies which are regarded as promoting separatist politics will encourage a move towards a kind of policy that is more Enlightenment-rationalist than *modus vivendi*. National newspaper headlines that constantly alert the British population to these types of immigrants or policies could be interpreted as encouraging such a move.

There is perhaps an inherent unfairness to this debate. For example, the focus upon cultural diversity as a form of differentiation that could challenge the bonds of togetherness required for the continuation of the welfare state ignores other forms of differentiation which also require some specific attention. For example, there is an increasing need for support of carers and of a rapidly-growing elderly population. Questions are being asked about the relevance of the state as it applies to this changing demographic, yet these questions are not being criticised for challenging support for the welfare state itself.[22] This issue does not arise. Instead, the welfare state is readjusted in order to make it more able to meet the needs of its population. The focus by Goodhart, therefore, on ethnic difference is troubling. Ann Phillips notes this problematizing of culture in relation to honour killing and contrasts this with the lack of attention given to the weekly killing of wives and girlfriends by husbands and boyfriends. The latter are individual aberrations and not problems of culture.

There is also a tragic dialectic that lies at the heart of this debate. The problem, if it is a problem, emerges as a form of identity politics which ruptures the previous consensus. The identity politics then is challenged for its essentialism yet at the same time the culture that is the source of the identity politics is problematized as a way of refusing its demands. But this pathologisation of its culture only strengthens its politics and so the tension and the distance increases. At a time when identity politics as a whole is reassessing its nature and form of protest, this kind of problematization of culture will only serve to increase the veracity of the politics which the state can seek to deny.

7 From Cultural Awareness to Cultural Competence

Thank you, and may I begin by expressing my appreciation to the organisers for inviting me to speak today. It is an honour to speak in support of this charity 'Helping Our Elders' and I would like to thank the organisers for providing me with an opportunity to make a case for cultural competency in public service delivery.[1]

In the next 15 minutes, I want to talk about difference and the recognition of difference in public service delivery. I want to say that recognising such difference makes us stronger and more effective.

But let me begin with the nature–culture distinction. Anthropologists and sociologists have noted how the modern individual separates himself or herself off from nature and culture.[2] And yet, despite this process of distancing, we have been able to cross the boundary between the individual and nature – that is, realise our connectedness, as the ecological crisis has forced us to examine our relation with nature. Other processes of modernity have forced us to consider our relation with humanity as a whole – and even within the boundary of the nation-state as we are repeatedly asked: 'How do we deal with difference?'

Steven Spielberg has offered us the choice between Jaws and ET. The other, as the nightmarish shark, attacking us while we are on holiday. Or the other, as cuddly alien, to be embraced and protected from the evil that lurks within ourselves. Sometimes, the difference can be assimilated through the annihilation of the source of that difference, and sometimes it is assimilated through its exaggeration. So, it is not only about how people are, it is also about how we perceive them, and then how that perception affects our relation to them. Migration, travel, globalisation and the information revolution will force us to address these questions again and again in the coming years. And we, as a nation, and as individuals will have to decide how we respond.

This city is a multicultural city with its settled migrants, its new migrants and its hybrid cultures – will also have to make decisions along the way as to how it responds to the challenges of difference. In my preparation for this speech, I assumed that increasing diversity is unique to this city but it seems that this is not the case. Amsterdam, Frankfurt, Birmingham, Paris, London and Marseilles are all very diverse and, as such, these considerations that I will tackle in this speech are not unique to this city but rather will need to be considered by policymakers across Europe.

I want to say at the outset that I don't believe that it is correct or appropriate to provide an absolutist position for all services and all situations in response to diversity. Instead, I would like to suggest that we should approach this question with an open mind – that is, a flexible toolkit, not a theory.

This is probably not the right place to explain in detail what such a toolkit should look like, but I would like to make a case for the principles that would underlie it.

The first question is difference according to whom? This question of difference, today, is not without its moral evaluation. And I should also say that we are living through a time of increased cultural racism – in other words, today, culture matters. Some people blame others because of their culture while others refuse to recognise culture in the delivery of services – so there is an informal recognition of cultural difference and a formal denial, sometimes simultaneously and by the same individuals. Sometimes it is much easier to make a change to policy that involves the recognition of culture in a negative way. Policy on forced marriage and preventing violent extremism come to mind. This is thought to be much easier to defend. The question of the recognition of culture is, therefore, a vexed one. Sometimes, the recognition of culture can be neutrally received whilst on other occasions it can cause discomfort to service providers and communities. This discomfort should not be a cause for ignoring the issue, rather the discomfort should encourage a policy of working in partnership through which the service providers and communities can come together to help deliver on shared agendas.

For example, adverse health outcomes may be due to cultural differences that are evaluated as morally neutral, or which are evaluated as morally negative. Either way, where the difference in health outcome is severe, it will require some form of working in partnership.

First of all, about cultural awareness. This is about the awareness of difference. It is about recognising that not all consumers or customers – in the current lexicon of public service delivery – are the same. Some consumers like fizzy drinks, and some consumers like juices. Choice is in fact the core principle of the market. And at present, the argument is that it is consumers who should decide how they receive their services. This does make some sense, and can certainly be supported by the principle of equality. But how should the state – and in this case the local state – recognise and then deliver services based upon cultural choice?

Perhaps, as I am asking these rhetorical questions, some of you may be thinking about the possibilities in which such service delivery may be inappropriate. I accept that the recognition of cultural difference in service delivery will be a matter of judgement for service planners and commissioners – for example, it may be appropriate and worthwhile to provide tailored services that recognise some cultural differences in relation to diabetes whereas it may not be worthwhile to recognise cultural difference in other situations, for example, in relation to asthma. What I am suggesting here is that extremist positioning in relation to service delivery – that is that we should ignore all forms of cultural recognition or that we should adjust for cultural differences in every situation – is less than satisfactory.

Ignoring all forms of cultural difference is a mistake. For example, to disregard differences in diet when dealing with obesity or diabetes is simply unprofessional. Similarly, to search for cultural differences in relation to the distribution of certain types of cancer or muscular diseases is probably not a useful exercise either, and certainly the research evidence would state so. So the first aspect of cultural awareness is to recognise the difference, where appropriate. And this may not be easy, for as Nietzsche says 'We hear the music of foreigners badly'.

What happens if we ignore cultural difference? Or perhaps more pertinently, can we ignore cultural difference? I would like to suggest two reasons why we cannot ignore cultural difference. First of all, strong cultures are already alive and well in many European cities. To ignore them is to pretend that they don't exist. Many people freely wish to belong to such cultures and many people reluctantly continue their participation in such cultures, so exit is not a realistic option for them. The development of the choice agenda in public services will have to consider whether it means choice according to the consumer or choice according to the state. Secondly, these cultures if unregulated can permit abuse within their midst and this leads eventually to the state having to adopt some form of formal recognition of the problem anyway, albeit by default.

But to move from cultural awareness to cultural competence is to move from the point of recognising difference to the point of redesigning services to not only accommodate that difference but in fact to provide a better service, and, for public services, this can mean that the service becomes more equitable and more efficient.

'Helping Our Elders' is an example of a service for South Asians afflicted by a disease that transcends culture. But, by recognising the patients' cultures, your charity has extended the reach of the service to people who were not being served by it. Previously, they were not receiving the same services as everybody else.

Is this charity the exception to the rule? Or should it be the norm? Let us look at the government's white paper 'Our Health, Our Care, Our Say' which states that 'health inequalities are still much too stark – across socioeconomic groups and in different communities requiring targeted, innovative and culturally sensitive responses.'[3]

In the section: 'Our vision for social care for adults in England', it states:

> Services should be person-centred, seamless and proactive. They should support independence, not dependence and allow everyone to enjoy a good quality of life, including the ability to contribute fully to our communities. They should treat people with respect and dignity and support them in overcoming barriers to inclusion. They should be tailored to the religious, cultural and ethnic needs of individuals. They should focus on positive outcomes and well-being, and work proactively to include the most disadvantaged groups. We want to ensure that everyone, particularly people in the most excluded groups in our society, benefits from improvements in services.[4]

The paper also recognises that market forces affect the uptake of service delivery. On GP practices:

> If the public has a choice of practices, then those that offer the most appropriate and responsive services will attract more patients. Practices will have to identify and meet the cultural and demographic needs of the population they serve – they will have to design services around the user in order to attract them.[5]

I would like to provide three examples of culturally competent services.

Let us begin with pain management. The pain management team at a local hospital were teaching patients who had recent-ly suffered a sudden illness how to manage their pain through generic techniques. They found that self-management was low amongst their Muslim patients. These same patients would then return home, and since many of them prayed, they would tolerate the pain through the positions of prayer. The team decided to teach the self-management of pain through the prayer movements. They found that this helped to increase the numbers of patients who continued to manage their pain after being discharged from hospital. A simple alteration or redesign of a service that helped to improve the quality of care.

Another more challenging example is the relation between psychiatry and spirituality. Some people are being misdiagnosed because of a lack of recognition of the role of spiritual beliefs in people's lives – references to *jinn* (spirit possession), for example, are regarded as a form of insanity. Local mental health practitionars have led in this area by showing how some accommodation of the different belief systems can help alleviate distress and suffering. In this situation, refusing to acknowledge difference can severely add to an individual's suffering. The project has been given national recognition and won several awards.

Finally, let me give an example from speech and language therapists who have found that using both English and Punjabi languages, for example, as teaching vehicles can help reduce the amount of language delay in some children who have been referred to the speech and language therapy team.

Cultural competence, ladies and gentleman, is about consideration, where appropriate. This charity is another example of care and consideration. By providing support for sufferers of Alzheimer's disease in the relevant language and in a culturally-appropriate manner, this charity has succeeded in extending the reach of social care services to a population that has been previously ignored.

I would like to reiterate that I am calling for a toolkit, not a theory. Tariq Modood, one of the leading political theorists in this area, points towards such a toolkit when he states:

This institutional architecture cannot be and should not be determined in advance but will grow through dialogue and social change and no doubt will result in something pragmatic, contingent, ramshackle and in what I call in my book, borrowing a term from elsewhere, a 'variable geometry'.[6]

Let me end by returning to Nietzsche who said:

> It is more comfortable for our eye to react to a particular object by producing again an image it has often produced before than by retaining what is new and different in an impression: the latter requires more strength, more 'morality'. To hear something new is hard and painful for the ear; we hear the music of foreigners badly.[7]

Ladies and gentleman, recognising difference is a sign of strength and I congratulate you for your vision and strength of purpose in supporting this project.

8 Finding a Saviour for a City in Need

Bradford is the cruellest city. It breeds lilac from the dead land. It's been a strange couple of weeks and I don't know if we made the right decision. Khan won't let go of it. He keeps on telling me I've colluded, that I've made a big mistake. But every time I think about it, I can only say that we did actually come to the right conclusion. We had a difficult time of it: we had to appoint a community cohesion manager for Bradford District Council and this was just after the Bradford riots. The problem was that we didn't know what community cohesion was or is. We agreed though that we were going to appoint 'a fixer'. Someone who was going to solve our problems – that's what we think community cohesion means – solving the city's problems after we'd just experienced the riots. The atmosphere was heated, and the debate sharp. There seemed to be a consensus in the city though. Multiculturalism had gone too far. The Pakistani community had been tolerated for far too long, there needed to be some kind of crackdown. And I hope that we've appointed the right man for the job. We interviewed the applicants yesterday.

There were four of us on the panel. The panel consisted of Frank, Deirdre, Asad Khan and me. Frank is the local inter-faith advisor to the city. He'd been here for a couple of decades, and built up a reputation as an expert on the city and its Muslim population. He came highly recommended and he'd contacted me before we met as a panel 'to have a chat' over a coffee. I was certainly impressed with his knowledge of the local Muslim community. Deirdre is a former lecturer in Justice Studies at the local university who now works as the main policy officer in this area for the Council. She will be line managing the new appointee. Asad is a primary school headmaster who has a reputation for being a bit of a race activist. I'd received a couple of calls about him from people whom he must have antagonised in the past. I was brought in as an outsider – 'an objective pair of eyes' as Deirdre had said. I work for a community centre as a manager in a nearby town. I'm known to the Muslim community, but also liked by the Council.

We were due to meet a week before we shortlisted the candidates. I hadn't been to Bradford in a long time and so I set off early. I drove down Leeds Road towards the city centre that sits at the base of a bowl, surrounded by the countryside or, as they say here, the moors. How apt is that? Bradford – a city besieged with problems – is surrounded by the moors. It was early in the afternoon and I looked down towards the city and the city hall clock tower that rose above the city: it was a beautiful sight. I pulled over and looked out the car window. The soft yellow on the horizon, the gentle green of the moors touching the soft yellow, and the yellow sandstone emerging from the centre of the city – lilacs from dead land. I looked down upon this city and its great beauty and its contradictions, I felt excited because of its beauty and yet bewildered at the same time. I saw some young men walk past. I felt afraid. I don't know why I felt afraid, but I remember the fear itself. I drove on towards the city centre.

The meeting was in one of the local council buildings. The council is based in two main buildings: one a nineteenth-century city hall that is based on Italian Gothic architecture and has to be one of the most beautiful buildings in the city. The other is a 1960s monstrosity: straight lines, squares, concrete – dullness objectified. We were meeting in Dullness HQ. I walked into the room. I was about 20 minutes early and Frank was already there.

'Hello Frank.'

'Hi Faisal.' He was busy flicking through his papers. 'There's some coffee if you like.'

I wandered over to make some coffee. 'So we're deciding on the questions today?', I asked.

'That's right, did you get the provisional list from Deirdre?'

'Yes, I did. I'm okay with all of the questions. This is going to be an important appointment.'

'Yes, we must get the right person in.'

'Do you know how many people have applied?'

'Yeah, I think it's 16.'

'Sixteen? What's the salary again?'

'I think about 40,000.'

Deirdre walked into the room at this point. 'Hi Frank, hi Faisal. You both well?' She placed her expensive-looking handbag on the table and made herself a cup of coffee. She had a multi-coloured scarf around her neck; it looked multicultural. 'Where's Asad?'

'I haven't seen him yet', said Frank.

'Okay, have you both had a chance to look at the questions? What did you think?'

Asad walked in at this point. 'Hi everyone.'

'Hi Asad, we're just about to start going through the questions.'

'Hi Asad,' said Frank, 'It's been a long time. Good to see you again.'

'Hi Frank.' I don't know if it was just me but there was something very cold between Frank and Asad, like an icy, invisible handshake.

'Right, let's start working our way through the questions. So, the first question is a general introductory question on the riots and their individual stance on the riots, what their response is etc.? Is that okay?' We all nodded. Deirdre continued. 'The next few questions are on the riots themselves: the police, the Muslim community and the media – about how they responded and what they should have done.'

'That sounds fine to me', I replied. Asad was quiet and staring at the table. He had an intense presence, but he also seemed very far away – elsewhere.

'We then have a question on the role of the political parties and finally a general question on their main priorities if they were to get the post. Okay, is everybody happy with that? Alright. I've brought the application forms with me and thought that we could perhaps shortlist the candidates.' She pulled out the application forms. Deirdre had a strange face: there had been some kindness there a long time ago, but years of bureaucracy had taken their toll and it looked as if the kindness had long departed from the contours of her face.

We proceeded to work through the 16 applications and eventually ended up with three candidates for interview whom we were to see the following week. The first candidate for interview was Mary Green. Mary had been engaged in community work for about three years, she had run discussion groups between community centres and was partially successful in building relationships between community centres in different parts of the city. She was in her mid-thirties and was well-known to Frank: they'd worked together on projects in the past. The second candidate for interview was Tahir Khan. Tahir was a Labour protégé. He had a youth work background and had helped to get young men into employment. The expectation was that one day he would become a councillor. The third candidate for interview was Nadeem Choudhury. Nadeem was the manager of a youth support programme that had received funding from the National Youth Agency. He was a practising Muslim and one who had been involved in his local mosque since his early teens.

We gathered a week later and interviewed the candidates. We asked the candidates how they interpreted the riots. The first question of the interview was, 'Imagine you are on *Newsnight*, the riots have just happened, I am Jeremy Paxman, how can you help us get out of this mess?' There was a clear polarisation between the candidates here. Mary and Tahir blamed the Pakistani community. They said that it was living in an alternative universe, segregating around its institutions and businesses. It didn't want to integrate. It wanted to maintain its own culture, worse, it was building up some romantic picture of what its culture was like 50 years ago in Pakistan and was trying to replicate it here. The children couldn't speak English properly, were not familiar with the local culture, and had become aggressive because violence is a part of the chauvinism that they were trying so hard to recreate.

It was quite painful listening to them sometimes. I couldn't help thinking when Mary was speaking that she was beginning to sound like some anti-immigration activist. And Tahir reminded me of that phrase used against Jews that criticise their own community: 'self-hating Jews' – was he a self-hating Pakistani? It certainly felt like it at times.

Nadeem though was very different in his explanation of the riots. He blamed the lack of economic opportunities that were available. 'I've got six friends, all graduates, can't get jobs – even really simple jobs. And then I meet people in good positions and it's no wonder that we have a problem. There's been a historic period of exclusion here in terms of plans and people, that's why we're in this mess.' This became a constant theme throughout the interviews as two broad paradigms emerged: one that blamed the community and the other that blamed the institutions.

A clear difference emerged here between the interviewers. Frank and Deirdre were both in agreement with Mary and Tahir, whereas Asad was with Nadeem. The second question of the interview was more specifically about the aggression of the South Asian young men. Why were they becoming more aggressive? Nadeem was clear on this. He said it was wrong to point to South Asian men as more aggressive. The street had just become a more dangerous and unwelcoming place and to say that Asian men were more aggressive was to interpret this problem through the prism of cultural difference. 'The street has taken on the law of the jungle and you have to walk with your chest out to survive. These young men act aggressively to protect themselves.' Mary said that they were angry: angry against their parents, against their culture and wider society. She suggested that it was to do with their culture, that their culture could make them violent: 'We may need to look at Pakistani culture to see if there is anything specifically in this culture that makes their young men more violent.' I remember pausing for thought, or was it shock, at this point: I was familiar with the Pakistani community in Manchester and this certainly didn't apply to them.

The next question was about the police and their response. Again the answers were polarised. Tahir said that the police had done a great job. They had protected the city and kept the rioting to a minimum. Nadeem though had criticised the police. He criticised their tactics on the day and he made a telling point in noting how few South Asian officers there still were in the force in Bradford. 'This made the riot into a colour thing,' he said, 'Pakistani youngsters and white policemen.' This was one of the few times when Deirdre and Frank both nodded in agreement with Asad.

A question followed about the media's reporting of the riots. There was an interesting and nuanced difference in the answers to this question. In terms of content, all the interviewees gave the same answer: the media coverage was exaggerated and unfair, and followed a pattern of painting the Bradford Muslim as some type of anti-citizen and Bradford as a city in which multiculturalism had gone horribly wrong, because it had gone too far. This was the media story and journalists were criticised by all the interviewees for their lazy depictions and easy stereotypes. The difference between the interviewees was in the tone. Nadeem had a mixture of anguish and real anger about the media. Mary was quite peculiar in her response, for though she said the same as Nadeem, she said it in an 'I told you so' sort-of-way, smug and perhaps even a bit self-indulgent. There was a real clash between Frank and Asad when we were discussing the interviews about this. It was Asad who picked up the difference in tone and asked us whether we had picked up on it as well and what we thought about it. I hadn't noticed it at the time but then after thinking about it agreed that there was clearly a difference. But Frank and Deirdre disagreed and Frank in particular became quite angry as if he was personally being attacked. Frank said that this was the reality that Bradford faced and the media should not be blamed for reporting what had actually happened. Asad said that the media angle had contributed to the riots by setting up Bradford as a strained place and added to the riots itself. The media were a part of the riots, not just as observers. Frank wasn't agreeing to this and said that as long as Bradfordians continued to avoid the key problems that faced the city, and blamed others instead, then the problems would continue. This disagreement was another source of tension between Asad on the one side and Frank and Deirdre on the other.

The interviewees were also asked about political engagement and why these young men were not engaging with the political parties to solve their problems. Mary and Tahir again agreed and blamed Muslim youth groups for radicalising young South Asian men by telling them to keep away from political engagement. Nadeem though launched into a prolonged critique of the political parties in the city for having offered little political leadership for the city, for being shy of working constructively with local communities, and for engaging with the community through its network of elders as opposed to trying to engage with the upcoming second generation.

The final question was about what needed to be done. Nadeem's answer here was the most interesting. He highlighted what he called 'relationality' and 'reciprocity'. Relationality meant that it was important for the council and the local communities to recognise that by virtue of sharing the same geographical space, they were all related and that the way in which this relation could be strengthened was through reciprocity. It certainly was the deepest answer but he didn't offer any concrete examples of how this could be achieved. Mary instead gave the example of a schools linking project. She suggested that the way to improve the city's problems was to focus on pairing up school children for a day in every term so that they can get to know children from other communities as schooling within the public system had become ethnically divided.

The interviews had been conducted in a matter of fact way and this had meant that we had finished slightly ahead of schedule. We decided to proceed on to discuss the candidates. Immediately, it was clear as to who the interviewers wanted to appoint. Frank and Deirdre were set on Mary and Asad wanted Nadeem to be appointed. I was undecided. We worked through the candidates and scored them individually. They all came out with very similar scores: Frank and Deirdre had put Mary ahead, Asad had put Nadeem ahead and somehow I had put Tahir ahead. I went through my scoring to understand why and he seemed to be a consistent second best on most questions. We decided to discuss the candidates. Frank asked me what I thought of Mary. I said that I didn't think that she was a bad candidate but her suggestion of the school linking project as a solution was a problem for me. What was the point I asked of getting kids to meet each other one day a term when they will return to their school and parents for the rest of the year? And it was the parents who had the problem with cultural difference who were raising the kids, so how were we going to make a substantive intervention by focusing on the kids of these parents through a schools linking project? Frank looked dismayed with my answer. Deirdre tried to convince me otherwise, but I couldn't see how Mary – though she said the right kind of things – could somehow provide the kind of leadership that was required. This city needed leadership, not an apology. Asad tried to make a case for Nadeem but it was shot down fairly quickly by Frank. He said that Nadeem was an old-school race activist, and that now we needed someone who was post-multicultural. Asad looked like he knew that he didn't have a chance but he tried to convince me anyway. I liked Nadeem's answer on the police, he was right to focus on the need for more police officers from the ethnic minorities. But he was also too dismissive, and this worried me. Worse, I didn't think his language – of identity politics in the main – was going to be helpful at this juncture in the city. I asked 'What about Tahir?' Asad shrugged his shoulders as if to say it didn't matter who it was if it wasn't Nadeem.

'Nadeem will offer the kind of leadership we need,' he replied. Frank looked depressed as if he had spent the last three years preparing Mary for this role and now at this final hurdle he was being denied. But Deirdre looked interested. 'Yes, I think Tahir is a good option. He has the right approach.'

'You mean he's not angry,' said Asad.

'No, I mean he's got the right approach, He's seeking a language of engagement. He wants everyone to be involved together in rebuilding the city. He understands the problems of the youth, he's been a youth worker,' she replied.

'He's a Labour Party activist and they've killed politics in Bradford Central,' Asad retorted. Frank began to look interested, if only because Asad was so vehemently opposed to Tahir.

'Do you think he's a house Negro?' Frank asked.

'A what?' Asad replied.

'A house Negro? You know the term, Malcolm X, your leader used it.' I stared at Frank in shock.

'What!'

Frank was beginning to show more interest in Tahir.

'Look,' I said, 'let's return to Malcolm afterwards. Do we think that Tahir can pull this off? Will he make a difference?'

'Yeah, I think so,' said Frank.

'Yes, I think so too. I think that he will be the unity candidate. And because he's from the Muslim community then he will be accepted by them. Right, Asad?' Deirdre looked towards Asad as she asked him for his opinion.

'I don't think so.' Asad looked like he didn't care.

Frank interjected, 'So we have three votes for Tahir. Shall we proceed?'

I suddenly became unsure of myself. We were appointing Tahir far too quickly. But before I could say anything further Deirdre who was chairing the process began to fill in the forms.

She ended the meeting. 'Okay, thank you very much.' Asad shook his head and left.

I left the meeting fairly soon afterwards. Frank and Deirdre looked like they wanted to talk to each other. I went to the local mosque to pray. I walked in. It was an attractive building. The stone had been brought over from India, and the arches and calligraphy were magnificent. One huge piece of calligraphy in the central hall said: 'The slaves of the Merciful walk gently on the earth.' I think it's from the Qur'an. I made a point of praying there whenever I could. It's more City Hall than Dullness HQ and for that the ex-textile workers who had built this huge, beautiful building needed to be congratulated for their hearts. It was quiet as it was between the congregational prayer times. There were three elders sat near the front. One sat cross-legged in the first row. He had his head bowed. Another was standing next to the radiator on the left wall. He was staring out across the prayer hall. And a third was sitting a few rows from the front reading the Qur'an in quite a loud voice. I prayed and then turned around to see two young men sitting in the corner. I must have missed them when I walked in. I walked towards the door but then one of the young men came up towards me, 'Faisal?'

'Yes?'

'You were on the interview panel right?'

'Uh, yes.'

'So who have you appointed?'

'I'm sorry I can't say.'

'Have you forgotten me? I'm Saeed. From uni.'

'Oh yeah, Saeed, how are you doing?' I hugged him. 'Long time no see! How are you?'

'Fine, thanks. Come and meet Riz.' I walked over and met Riz. He was now standing near the exit of the mosque. They had prayed and were about to leave. They may have been waiting to talk to me. I knew Saeed from our university days. We were both in the same halls of residence. He was a hard-working and conscientious student, but not that politically active. Riz was a school friend of his, they had both gone to university and returned to work in the city. They were impressive: articulate, angry, interested and interesting. I received a text from Deirdre who told me that the news of the appointment had been leaked to the local press and was going to be in the evening paper. She told me to be prepared. And just on cue Saeed asked: 'So who have you appointed?' Bradford can at times be a very small place.

'We've appointed Tahir,' I replied.

'Tahir? Tahir! What about Nadeem?' Saeed wasn't happy.

'Nadeem? No, we didn't appoint Nadeem,' I tried not to show any emotions on my face.

'What about Nadeem, he's much better than Tahir,' Riz joined in. I was surprised by how much they both knew about the appointment and the candidates, word must have got out.

'Look I can't talk about the process. Do you know either of them?'

'Do we? The whole city knows Tahir and Nadeem and you've appointed Tahir. What a disaster!' Riz was quite straightforward. I had become used to this bluntness that is common amongst some Bradfordians. They prefer to call it honesty.

I asked Riz: 'Do you know Nadeem?'

'Yes, he got us off the streets,' he replied.

'Tahir's got people off the streets as well.' I had heard of some of the work that Tahir had done with young men just down the road from this particular mosque.

'Tahir's got himself off the streets.' Saeed wasn't convinced.

'That's a good outcome, though, isn't it?,' Riz interjected. They both smiled at each other and shook their heads at the same time.

Saeed responded: 'Yeah, less stupidity on the streets ... I can't believe you didn't appoint Nadeem. That's another five years wasted.'

I became slightly angry and felt the need to defend myself: 'What do you mean wasted? Nadeem was the wrong man for the job.'

Riz replied straight away: 'Nadeem understands the issues.'

I dug my heels in. 'Nadeem would have made things worse. He would increase segregation.'

Saeed looked at me quizzically: 'What segregation?'

I tried to hold my ground: 'You know, the self-segregation that's happening here in Bradford.'

Saeed began to look slightly angry and crossed his brow as he asked: 'What do you mean segregation?'

I responded: 'Well, some people are saying that Muslims are trying to make this into a Muslim area. Some people have been threatened. Had rubbish thrown into their garden. This place looks like it's segregated.'

'Most people leave because they don't want to live near Pakis,' Riz replied. They were familiar with this argument. 'Our families have got bigger and everyone else has moved out. We've just got bigger as a community, that's all. That's why it looks like there's more of us. What we need is more jobs and better education for our kids. Tahir won't help us get jobs. He'll tell us to mix once a month with some white folk. What an idiot!'

Saeed added: 'He's gonna blame us you know. Be better citizens, be better Muslims, he'll say. I can see his point but he's not a preacher. His job is to help our community with opportunities.'

I asked Saeed: 'Isn't that what needs to be done? Hasn't he got a point? Doesn't the Muslim community need to get its own house in order?'

Saeed answered as if he had given this answer many times before. 'Yes, but we've been complaining to everyone about this for years. No one wants to help us and at the same time they keep on blaming us.'

Riz added: 'Anyway, Tahir can't keep on blaming us for not doing anything. We've been working on the Employment Outreach project for two years now. How many people have we helped into jobs so far?' He looked at Saeed.

'Twenty-six,' said Saeed.

'Twenty-six?' I was surprised.

'Yeah.'

'What, 26 young Muslims into jobs, how did you do that?' I wanted to know more.

Riz was surprised I didn't know about this. 'No, not Muslims, we went to the white estate just down the road and set up an office there. We go there twice a week for three hours each evening to help with school work and job applications. We've helped 26 people into work. Not great jobs, but at least they're in work.'

'That's amazing, well done.' I was impressed.

Saeed though wanted to talk about problems in the Muslim community. 'But we need to change things here as well. You come on a Friday here and listen to the Friday *khutba*. Look at the audience, there's no connection. People are just performing the motions. We have a body without substance. It's hollow. We ask the mosque committee for a sermon in the English language and they tell us to be careful or the imams might take over. Look at the committee. Half of them own *haram* businesses. Look at Mr Khan. He's treasurer of the mosque committee and he runs a claims firm. What kind of religion is this?'

'It's religion without morality,' Riz answered Saeed's question, 'Hollow religion.'

Saeed continued: 'But the youth are confused, they're searching for some structure, the street is unforgiving and powerful. It waits like a hungry animal ready to devour any weakened or empty soul that dares to tread into its territory. This mosque isn't providing it. We're failing our brothers, and our children. I blame our fathers.'

'How?'

'They came here, they didn't think about us then. They say they built these mosques for us and our children, but they didn't: they built it for themselves. This is their home from home. Their peace and quiet. They don't see that we need the mosque as well, we need the *khutba*. Our children do, the women do. But they keep on saying that that's not our way. They brought us here. They raised us here, sent us to English schools, turned the TV on to keep us quiet, told us to go to university to get an education. And they don't have an imam that can speak English. What did they expect? That we would be raised in Britain and be anything other than British? And now they've got Tahir who'll talk the talk but he will do the whole thing again. Watch.'

Riz continued on from Saeed. It looked like they had discussed this many times before. 'They don't care about us. Look at Mr Salim. His son is in jail. He is on the mosque committee and he pretends that he doesn't understand the issues. I know he cries about his son. You can see it in his eyes, but he won't change anything, he's too proud, too stubborn.'

Saeed gave another example. 'Look at Mr Abdul. He's got two daughters, both bright. Both moved away from their parents. They spent two years trying to get our mosque to open up to women. And now they're disheartened and he wants them to marry his nephews in Pakistan. Both went to uni, one is a psychologist and the other a dentist. Which world is he living in?'

Riz was getting emotional. 'The elders are in denial. They deny the fact that they ever came here. They pretend that they are still in Pakistan. Their kids have left them, are in crime, in jail, unemployed, but still they pretend that everything is okay. We need some change. Someone has to stand up. Sometimes I think that they hate us, they don't love us, care for us, or want the best for us. No, they hate us.'

'Who do you turn to? What about the councillors?' I asked them.

Saeed then brought it back to today's appointment. 'They play along with it. Tahir is Mr Khan's nephew. You've given him a job now but one day he'll be a councillor, an MP even, and may join the mosque committee. The cycle will continue. The parties don't care about this: they'll go to the media though when it suits them, telling them how bad we are. They all serve each other. The committees, the councillors, the parties, the council, the police etc. It's all one big happy family. Tahir's just saying the right things, but he won't change anything. Nadeem was challenging: that's why people don't like him. He asked the hard questions of the councillors, the council, the elders and that's why he's a loner. You should have appointed him. All Tahir does is talk about self-segregation, how we're not integrated, don't want to integrate.'

Tahir was not an uncontroversial character. He had previously been chair of the local Race Equality Council. But the committee had asked him to leave because he was seen to be soft on racism; this is what had endeared him to Frank and Deirdre. However, he had only agreed to support the Race Equality Council chair if he was made chair. 'Why did he agree to become chair of the anti-racial organisation after he said that he wasn't going to join?' They were beginning to ask questions with an increasing feeling of anger. It was as if they were operating as a tag team. As one finished asking his question, the other began his. 'Is his consultancy still gaining contracts from work aligned with his anti-racial campaigns?'

'Anti-racist', I corrected Riz.

'Anti-whatever, you know what I mean.'

Tahir had a race equality consultancy which was found to have won contracts after he had successfully campaigned against the college's treatment of Pakistanis while acting as chair of the Race Equality Council. I knew about this and knew that Tahir had refused to answer this question when asked by another friend of mine, I overlooked it because this is how most people worked in this area.

Riz was in full flow by now. 'He shifted his position from being pro-equality to being pro-cohesion. What brought about the change apart from the new job? I remember he came here to this mosque about a couple of years ago and spoke about nothing but racism and then a couple of weeks later he was there in the council telling the council committee how Pakistanis were to blame for poor educational standards in the city. And Tahir's our new community cohesion manager for the city, three cheers for the city leaders who make these decisions.'

They looked at me and truth be told I didn't have an answer. I said I'd look into it, but I don't know what that meant to them or even if they had heard it. I walked back to my car and drove home. It had been a long day and the sun was setting over the city. Bradford is the cruellest city, it breeds lilacs but does not give them space to grow. It is dead land and yet it gives life.

It sometimes feels as if Bradford is at a perpetual crossroads. As if the future is always waiting to be written in a single moment which weighs so heavily upon the city. If I have one form of consolation, it is that this is not true. These moments will not determine the future, Bradford will not stand condemned by these moments, but instead a city of this size and complexity will turn the corner and grow and mature and perhaps the mistakes will occur less and less. Maybe we made one mistake today, time will tell. In the meantime, the sun will continue to rise and fall on this city, as everyone continues to live their lives as best they can. As I left Bradford, I stared at the horizon as the sun was setting and it was a mixture of dark yellows, light greens and light blues as the Yorkshire stone met the green grass and the blue sky in this most extraordinary city.

9 Farewell to the Bush Years

So long – take thy flight!
No longer stay in sight!
Much converse do I find in thee,
Historian of our infamy![1]

What do you remember of the Bush years?

It probably is still too early to tell and this may be an exercise in wishful thinking but one can only hope and pray that now that George W. Bush has left office that we can perhaps say goodbye to what might be characterised as 'the Bush years'. It's difficult to remember the Bush years except as one long, enduring, painful moment that will not go away. At various times, different aspects of it rise to the surface to heighten the pain and these may then go away but the pain nevertheless remains. We were left feeling numb and powerless while nothing seemed clear or visible except that we were vulnerable and under attack. Subject to fate, we hoped that there would not be another terrorist attack and yet simultaneously watched anti-Muslim politicians, writers and journalists take unfair advantage of this situation as we succumbed to our shared depressed state. The Bush years – specifically from 11th September 2001 to 14th November 2008 when Barack Obama was elected – can be remembered as one massive fuzzy haze. If Dickens said that the time of revolution was the worst of times and the best of times then it felt like this now as well. Yes, it was the worst of times. But at the same time many things happened that suggested it could be the beginning of something better.

It was the worst of times because we felt humiliated and cornered. So many people have died, Muslims and non-Muslims. In the frenzy of the continuous chain of events, we have probably lost count of who died and where. There were so many incidents. The Mumbai massacre in which terrorists attacked major hotels in Mumbai in India killing 173 people. The riots in Gujarat in India in which over 790 Muslims and 254 Hindus were killed after some Muslims had burned a train killing 59 passengers. The bombing in Bali which killed over 200 people, many of them tourists, at a nightclub. The killings in Jenin in which over 50 Palestinians were killed by Israeli soldiers. The fall of Saddam Hussain from being one the strongest leaders in the Arab world to someone who went into hiding and then was caught and executed. The second intifada that included the return of suicide bombings to Israeli soil and the assassination of the Hamas leadership in Gaza by Israel. The arrests of hundreds of Arabs in the States in the aftermath of the 9/11 attacks. The increasing use of expanding powers through legislation as a response to the war on terror which now includes being able to hold people up to 28 days before they must be released. The practice of 'extraordinary rendition' which actually meant the kidnap and then transportation of individuals across the world, sometimes to places where they were handed over to third parties whom were known to use torture. The takeover of a school in Beslan by Chechen separatists and the consequent murder of 186 children in that school. The portrayal of the Prophet Muhammad in a series of cartoons published in a Danish national newspaper that were then published around the world, and which lead to mass rioting in many parts of the world resulting in more than a 100 deaths. The ban of 'ostentatious religious symbols' in France which meant that Muslim girls could not wear the hijab at school. The associated ban in certain German states on wearing the hijab in public places. The rise of Pym Fortuyn as a Dutch political leader and his subsequent assassination. The assassination of Theo Van Gogh, a Dutch film director, who had produced an offensive film about Islam. The rise of the far right across Europe which specifically focused on the Muslim community as the source of contention whether it was Jean Marie le Pen in France or Jorg Haider in Austria. The invasion of Afghanistan and Iraq. The death of Dr David Kelly and the Hutton enquiry into his death. Robin Cook's speech against the impending invasion of Iraq. The debate on the Sharia in Britain and more specifically the Archbishop of Canterbury's comments that the Sharia was 'inevitable' in Britain. The 7th July bombings in London in which over 50 people were killed. The niqab (face-veil) debate in Britain in which a senior politician asked for Muslim women to remove their niqabs as he felt it was not appropriate in British public life. The bombings of trains in Madrid in which over 200 people were killed by Moroccan terrorists. The capture of John Walker Lindh who became known as 'the American Taliban' and is now in a high security American prison serving 20 years for taking up arms against the United States. The setting up of special camps at Guantanamo Bay which were outside any global legal scrutiny. The pictures that emerged from Abu Ghraib prison of the torture that had taken place there. The many trials of Muslim suspects including Dhiren Barot, Richard Reid, and Saajid Badat in which the Muslim suspects were found guilty and the many trials of Muslim suspects in which they were released either by the jury or on appeal. The shooting of a young Muslim man in Forest Gate as police raided his home and the shooting of a young Brazilian who was mistaken for a suicide bomber by police at the Stockwell Tube Station. The many terrorist attacks in Iraq against the invasion and the battle in Fallujah which was fierce but unreported by the Western media. The building of the Israeli wall to divide up Israel from the West Bank and the bombing and invasion of Gaza by Israeli forces in which over 1400 people were killed. This is some of what has happened during the Bush years and it is difficult to remember it all, though every aspect of it is important. Collectively, it will be remembered as a very difficult period.

What were the lowest moments?

Everyone will think back to their own worst moment during the Bush years. For me, it was in 2004. The bombings in Madrid meant that terrorism had become a possibility on European soil within a post-9/11 context. This was a major development for European Muslim communities and the British Muslim community. The siege of the school in Beslan was in 2004. A second intifada was fully underway and Israel had described its continuing occupation as its own version of 'the war on terror'. I was disturbed by the assassination of the Hamas leadership: this was extra-judicial killing, and many times, several innocent bystanders were killed in the assassinations as well but this was never mentioned. British counter-terrorism strategy was poorly developed and there was hardly any communication with the Muslim community. The Prevent strand was non-existent and at the time the Pursue strand was run by people who had very little knowledge of the new threat and how to deal with it. British Muslim parliamentarians then were Mohammad Sarwar and Khalid Mahmood and both were incapable of providing leadership to the community. The Muslim Council of Britain had been vociferous in the national media but had very little reach into the community itself. The blogs, websites and satellite channels that we have now were all absent then. The Hutton enquiry into the death of Dr David Kelly had reported in the early part of the year. Dhiren Barot was arrested in the middle of the year and sentenced for seven years for conspiring to cause terrorist attacks in the United States. Iraq had been invaded in the previous year and most of 2002 had been spent in the run-up to the Iraq war but in 2004 this now looked like it was not going to be a matter of one major terrorist attack followed by an invasion of two countries, instead it was at this point looking like it was turning into a major clash of two civilisations. And there were very few people crossing the divide. If François Burgat had spoken about 'bilateral radicalisation' in

North Africa between the state and the jihad movement, then this was bilateral radicalisation on a global scale.[2] At least, it began to feel like it was and there was no end in sight. But most worrying of all were two facts that are perhaps related. The first was the response of some Muslims to the killings of school children in Beslan: a shrug of the shoulders: 'they killed many Chechen children, the Chechens are killing their children'. The second was the complete feeling of helplessness: 'events are beyond our control'. I didn't think then that there was a large group of people within the Muslim community who were intent on terrorist attacks, but I did feel that events were forcing our community into a politicised corner out of which we could only escape through more radicalisation.

How did you cope?

It became very difficult to cope. I think that many adopted an approach of cynicism towards the whole political situation. They saw it as a conspiracy or a planned attack against them and their faith. Others just continued with their lives with a sense of political anger while ignoring the events around them as if nothing was happening. Perhaps you could describe it as a learned political fatalism. I don't think that many have coped well with the Bush years; we'll know that when we look back in the future. At present, I don't know if anyone has done any work on how the Bush years affected employment prospects for the Muslim community or whether there were increased incidences of mental illness. Having said all of that, looking back now at where the community is today, I do think that the community has been fairly resilient and this has to be applauded, especially since the 7th July attacks.

How do you think the Muslim community responded to the 7th July attacks?

There was initially some shock, some denial and some defensiveness. We obviously didn't want it to be British Muslims who were behind this but as the news was released of the identities of the bombers then the community had to face up to the harsh facts. I don't think that anyone in the community expected there to be a terrorist attack in the UK by British-born Muslims. We certainly knew that there was a possibility of a terrorist attack. We knew that the invasion of Iraq made this more likely. But I didn't know of anyone who remotely called for such a terrorist attack. It would have been a fringe of a fringe, people unknown to others. And so it was.

I think this is one moment in which Tony Blair should be applauded for his leadership. He pulled, as Prime Minister, the Muslim community very close to him in the immediate aftermath of the attack by publicly inviting leaders to Downing Street and by making statements on television about not blaming the community. This was an important moment, and he acted as a leader should. The community was very clear in its condemnation of the attacks and this was important. It was after the 7th July attacks that the Prevent strand of British counter-terrorism began in earnest but then with this came the whole question of political representation and leadership of the community. This has been very problematic and strained and I can't say whether it has to this day been satisfactory resolved.

Why is that?

There is a central paradox at the heart of Britain's counter-terrorism strategy. The primary function of any counter-terrorism strategy should be the prevention of any terrorist attacks. Initially, this began as a co-ordination of approaches but as the Prevent strand gathered pace so spending commitments increased such that those that were helping in countering terrorism would begin to receive financial assistance – usually because it was logistically necessary. However, this then became a question of patronage, more specifically, who should the government support through its patronage? And further that the government should not support those that are deemed to be ambivalent on these issues or those that cannot be regarded as socially progressive. There is one line of argument that suggests that the government should only work fully with those that are totally clear in their rejection of terrorism and are socially progressive. The specific problem here is the influence of Islamist-inspired organisations on the Muslim Council of Britain (MCB) in particular. The government fairly soon after the 7th July attacks decided that it didn't wish to prioritise the delivery of its counter-terrorism strategy in the Muslim community through Islamist-inspired organisations. The question here then becomes whether this makes British counter-terrorism less effective. This remains a moot point.

Indirectly, it also becomes a debate about who should lead the Muslim community and because the Prevent strand seems to be the main point of contact between the British state and the Muslim community at present, then the outcome of this debate has profound consequences for the community and its holistic development. The government has tried to work with two rival organisations to the Muslim Council of Britain: the Sufi Muslim Council and the British Muslim Forum. Both have received considerable financial support and are still developing their infrastructure. And so it appears that though the community responded in a firm way to the 7th July attacks it does seem that the argument over political representation and recognition has sidetracked this development and it is difficult to say whether there has therefore been much progress since then, especially in the constituencies that matter. In fact, the government's behaviour over political recognition may have been counter-productive in that it may have helped to reduce goodwill from the Muslim community as a whole towards Britain's counter-terrorism strategy.

The other matter to consider is the Pursue strand of British counter-terrorism. This also had a chequered history during the Bush years. There have been some catastrophic errors such as the shooting of Jean Charles de Menezes, the arrest of Lotfi Raissi as a key link to the 9/11 hijackers, the arrest of 11 Pakistani nationals in 2009 on suspicion of being involved in a big terrorist plot and the failure to prevent actual terrorist attacks including the 7th July bombings and the 2007 terrorist attacks by two doctors. The Pursue strand has therefore made many errors of huge proportions. However, since it is in the main related to the activities of the security services then it cannot be subject to public scrutiny in the same way that matters related to the Prevent strand are. When reports are published such as the recent report from the Office for Security and Counter-Terrorism on arrests since 9/11, the Pursue strand comes under heavy criticism.[3] Two outstanding issues that remain seem to be the very slow pace at which the structure is being made fit for purpose and secondly the lack of involvement of Muslims in the scrutiny of the Pursue strand – one can only assume that this is because of a lack of trust. For example, the Office for Security and Counter-Terrorism was only very recently formed in the Home Office to supervise British counter-terrorism and Muslim involvement in the OSCT came at a very late stage of its organisational formation. The Pursue strand does need to be subjected to much more scrutiny.

What is your view on the Prevent strand as a whole?

Well, the first point I'd like to make is that there is has been too much focus on the Prevent strand and too little focus on the Pursue strand. 'Stakeholder engagement' was a necessary part of New Labour policy. Any area of work whether it be educational underachievement or mental health required some form of engagement with the people for whom the policy was intended. This applied more so in my view to British counter-terrorism. Furthermore, Prevent was necessary in the aftermath of the 7th July attacks not just because of engagement but also because in its absence it left the Pursue strand to itself which was the case up to 2005. The history of Prevent can be divided in to four stages.

The first stage was pre-Prevent, if you like. If we take 9/11 as the beginning (this could be disputed, because there was some activity in this area in the nineties), then there was a period which I find most astonishing up to July 2005 in which there was no Prevent. The second stage began after the bombings in July 2005. This included the forming of seven working groups of Muslims that were called to advise the government in different areas including regeneration, youth, education, mosques, extremism, women and security and policing. Many recommendations were presented to government and some of them were taken up although the government was criticised for not taking up more of the recommendations. The response was that many of the recommendations could not be taken up by government because it remained for the community itself to take them up.

The third stage was a response to the second stage. The problem with the second stage was that it involved activities at the national level and there was not enough devolution of the Prevent strategy to the local level, There needed to be productive partnerships at the local level for the Prevent strategy to work thoroughly. Councils with large Muslim populations were therefore chosen and given small amounts of money in the first trial year to examine how this process would play out. The problem was that many councils were distant from their local Muslim communities and their youth, sometimes due to exclusion and sometimes due to history. The government decided to roll out a three year programme of funding for Muslim community groups to work together with the local councils on the Prevent agenda.

This led on to the fourth stage. The police had a counter-terrorism remit which focused on the second strand of the government's anti-terrorism or 'contest' strategy: the Pursue strand which was about actually apprehending people who were about to commit terrorist attacks. It was about this time when British counter-terrorism as a whole was refashioned with local counter-terrorism units and the Office for Security and Counter-Terrorism at the Home Office being constituted. The fourth stage of Prevent involved the funding of Prevent strands specifically in police forces, sometimes aligned with the neighbourhood policing agenda. This was announced by government at the time.

Three recent reports have been published on the Prevent strategy that have criticized it. The first report was published by

Khalida Khan of the An-Nisa Society, the second was *Spooked* by Arun Kundnani of the Institute of Race Relations, and the third was published by the House of Commons Committee for Communities and Local Government which had launched an enquiry into Prevent in late 2009.[4] All three reports have made criticisms of the Prevent strategy but from different perspectives. Khalida Khan criticized the Prevent strategy from the perspective of a Muslim community third-sector organization that felt that the approach of the state towards the community should have been unrelated to any security agenda. An-Nisa Society had been calling for the recognition of the Muslim third sector for years and was disappointed that when the recognition finally came, it came through the preventing violent extremism strand. Arun Kundnani documented several incidences of overlap between the Prevent strand and surveillance and suggested that this was proving harmful to the Muslim community and its engagement with the state. The Communities and Local Government Committee made 27 recommendations in their report which examined issues such as the overlap between Prevent and Pursue, Prevent and community cohesion and the role of theology (*sic*) in deradicalisation.

Personally, my view is that while a threat of terrorism remains, then the Prevent strand is necessary to help reduce the threat and to counterbalance the Pursue strand. Certainly something like Prevent will remain in place, albeit in much reduced form, despite its formal scrapping by the new Conservative–Liberal Democrat coalition in July 2010.[5] If there have been difficulties or abuses along the way (as highlighted in the reports) then safeguards need to be put in place and one of the best safeguards seems to me to be Muslim involvement as scrutiny of both the Prevent and the Pursue strands. Anything to do with mainstreaming or third-sector activity should be treated as such and separated off from any Prevent functions (though they will clearly have Prevent-associated outcomes). But this is another challenge as well as officialdom has in practice been slow to recognize Muslim voluntary activities.

147

Going back to the Bush years and your experience of them. Did it feel like a war on Islam?

The immediate answer to your question is that yes, at times, it did feel like a war on Islam. And certainly many people that I spoke to said that they also felt like it was a war on Islam. That doesn't mean that I actually thought there was a war on Islam. This is because I could not understand what a war on Islam would entail. What would it look like? Would everyone have to stop reading the Qur'an? Would all biographies of the Prophet be called back? Would all Muslims have to openly refute their allegiance to the Islamic creed? This was obviously not the case. It was a war against some Muslims, namely those of the Jihad movement that have openly called for terrorist attacks. Some people have used this war as an opportunity to further their own ends and so have attached cultural anti-Muslim perspectives to the arguments, and it is this that has made it feel like a war against Islam.

Was it possible to ignore it?

It was impossible to ignore it. There had to be a concerted effort against any terrorist groups within the community. They had to be persuaded to change their minds, or if they were about to engage in a terrorist attack, then they had to be handed over to the police. After 2004, things began to take the form of a cycle. There would be a bad Muslim news event every three or four months, sometimes across the world. If it was quiet for too long, then you began to expect the next event. A war, an attack, or as began to happen, a bad news story about the lack of integration of Muslims into British society. This was an important development. Though several of us from within the community were constantly making the case for separating out the two policy areas of counter-terrorism and integration, there were others who were working to merge the two in the public mind to make one overriding narrative: the reason behind terrorist attacks is cultural isolation. To me, these were separate problems that are not empirically linked. Many people are culturally isolated but not politically motivated and many others are politically motivated but culturally integrated. However, in terms of a response from the community it was clear to me that we had to as a community make as many bridges with wider society as possible and across all levels of interaction: individual, family, community, local, regional, national, faith-based, political, academic, journalistic, male, female, old and young, left and right. I think many in the community began to adopt this as a counter-measure to the continuous media stories and it has certainly worked. Those who know Muslims are much less likely to be prejudiced against Muslims as a whole.

I'd just like to clarify my position here. I don't believe that cultural isolation is a cause of terrorism that is that I don't think that a lack of integration is the cause of the problem, but I do think that cultural integration can help reduce the possibility of terrorism because the more that Muslims are integrated then the less likely it is that they will attempt to attack the cities to which they feel they belong. As a note, I'd like to highlight here that I'm calling for an integration of difference and not the assimilation of sameness.

Who are the main voices of this site of resistance?

The other site of resistance has been the internet. And this is something that marks a dramatic and structural shift from previous situations in which Muslims were on the receiving end. E-mailing became an instant way of organising one's messages and mass distributing them. Websites that gathered and then published useful information became popular. Counter-narratives were quickly developed. Counter-examples were mass distributed. Blogs also began to appear at this stage and provided a site of resistance to any narratives in the national media that were overly demonising the community. The mainstream media has also moved over to the net so here in one sense a great equalisation has occurred. Though papers like the *Guardian* and the *Telegraph* still have huge resources to support their webpages, they are nevertheless all just one click away from every internet user as a blogger that gathers the argument and the evidence to challenge their positions. Interestingly, looking at the press, there are still very few Muslims who write for the mainstream press after so many years of extensive coverage of Muslim affairs. It is only the *Guardian* that has challenged this by opening up its 'Comment is Free' pages to many Muslim commentators and within the national press this is the place that one turns to read Muslim views on the political topic of the day.

I don't know how these things historically began but I would guess that it began with e-mailing a few friends which became an e-mail list that then developed into a website. This form of political activism was related to events. The officials no longer had a monopoly on the channels of communication. Where people felt frustrated with the official account of events they could link their contacts through e-mail to counter-narratives. This then developed into fully fledged websites. The prototypical example here is the Muslim Public Affairs Committee UK.[6] Bloggers have emerged as well as have numerous websites which describe political events and provide analysis.

What was the greatest moment?

The greatest moments were when the smallest rays of hope began to appear. One of the biggest problems was that the Muslim community was and perhaps remains so far away from being the least bit prepared for the challenges it faces. There is no national functioning organisation that can authoritatively present the community's case to government and wider society in an institutionalized and professional way. There are very few national leaders who command the respect of the community and of wider society. There seems to a real schism between religious and non-religious leaderships whether this is in business, academia or politics. There are hardly any functioning regional organisations and very few local organisations. In short, community leadership is severely dysfunctional. One of the reasons for this is the lack of unity or understanding what unity means or ought to mean for the community. In many senses, there is perhaps not even a sense of a unity of purpose for the community. Amidst all of this, when it seems that so much of what the community is doing is so wrong, the greatest moments came when it appeared that at least some sections of the community had managed to get it right. Sami Yusuf's first album launched in 2003 was one such example. Deenport.com as a web-based Muslim community that is culturally confidant and literate is yet another example of something the community has got right. The recent establishment of the Cambridge Muslim College in 2009 is another. Altrincham Muslim Association just outside Manchester and Madni Mosque in Bradford are offering model examples for other nascent Muslim institutions. The emergence of Salma Yaqoob as a political leader was another. These were moments when the rays of hope began to appear.

These are all important, but in terms of the grand scheme of things then the big turnaround was the election of Barack Obama to the office of the President of the United States of America. The most important moment for me here was the Iowa caucus. By the time of the presidential election itself it was clear there was a strong chance that Obama might become President. But it was at the Iowa caucus that this first became a possibility. It was said that a white state would never vote in an African-American for President so when Obama became the leading Democratic candidate in Iowa for President then this meant that for the first time in the campaign he was an actual possibility for President. Up to this point I had seen him as an interesting candidate and not much more. I didn't think that he had a chance. I'd seen his speech to the Democratic Convention in 2004 and he was a powerful young speaker, full of energy, though I wasn't sure where he was going with 'the promise of America'. I was far more interested, intrigued even, by his choice of Samantha Power as a foreign affairs advisor. I had been following Samantha Power's work since 9/11 as an American academic in the area of human rights who had made public interventions into the debates on human rights in the war on terror which contrasted with the interventions

151

of Alan Dershovitz and Michael Ignatieff.[7] All were based at Harvard University, and Power and Ignatieff were both based at the Carr Center for Human Rights. Ignatieff had made a case for the legitimacy of torture whereas Power was clearly against torture. But it was at the point that Obama became an actual possibility for President that must represent the greatest moment of hope for me during the Bush years, namely, that the Bush years might be coming to an end, and not in a slow, whimpering sort of way, but with a bang and an almost total reversal in policy. It was as if Obama was a possibility and could only have been a possibility because of the Bush years.

But hope is also spiritual. And I don't want it to sound as if hope and despair are entirely bound up with our material and political circumstance. Yes, it was very difficult to ignore the events that surrounded us. But the way of the religious person is to rest his hope in the eternal spring, and to let the immediate problems pass away because they too will pass as they did. In the life of the heart therefore there is this constant struggle between the immediate and the Eternal as one's quiet religious life is repeatedly violated if that is how it was felt by the immediacy of political events which were beyond the control or influence of most of us. Hope is always present for those with their eyes on Eternity, but the rapid rush of one event after another made it such that our gaze could not ignore what was beginning to happen around us in ever decreasing circles.

Did the war on terror affect you personally?

The war on terror in the main and for the majority of Muslims was a news event. By this, I mean that it affected others. Others were killed, tortured and arrested. The majority of Muslims were therefore not directly affected by the war on terror, except when it came to travel. Even here, many Muslims will have travelled during the Bush years without any difficulty. This was not however my experience. I was questioned on many occasions while crossing borders during the Bush years. I did feel that the war on terror gave immigration bureaucrats an excuse to pull me aside. On each occasion, and especially when I was pulled aside, I remember looking at the official who was asking me these questions and wondering whether he or she really was in a position to make an informed judgement as to my innocence. It seemed very arbitrary. I fitted the profile: a British Muslim of South Asian heritage, travelling.

I was stopped in Aqaba in Jordan as myself, my wife and my son returned from Nuwaiba in Egypt. We had crossed the border to visit Egypt and then renew our visa for Jordan. We had spent a day in Nuwaiba and had caught the fast boat – a hovercraft – back from Aqaba. We had taken the slow boat – large ferry – to Aqaba and the wait had been long and the journey slow so we had decided to take the fast boat back. We arrived in to Aqaba and were taken into immigration services. As the fast boat was that bit more expensive the majority of people on it were Americans, Europeans and Australians. We all sat down in the waiting area and were called up nationality by nationality by the immigration officials. When it came to the British, they began to call us by our names. Eventually, the only people remaining in the waiting area were us. I had said to my wife earlier that I did not expect us to leave Aqaba before the arrival of the slow boat, but I was half-joking at the time. And sure enough, the slow boat had appeared on the horizon. We waited. After about an hour, when the slow boat was much closer to the port we were called by a policeman who then asked us to follow him. He took us through offices, stairways and corridors to the office of the chief immigration official at the top of the port from which we could see the whole port. We were asked to wait outside. Eventually, a young man who was not that much older than me walked up to us and asked me to enter the office. I asked my family to remain outside as I went to answer the usual questions. The same young man sat at the main desk and asked me to take a seat. I sat down. And he proceeded in a very cold and angry way to ask me questions about what I was doing in Jordan and why I had visited Egypt. I told him that I was learning Arabic in Jordan and had visited Egypt for a holiday. He continued to ask me some questions, but after about five minutes an older man came in and tapped him on the shoulder. This older man then took the seat at the main desk as the younger man left. He continued to look through my passport and asked me the same questions again. After my third or fourth answer, he began to relax and asked me how life was in Britain. I told him it was alright. And the job situation in my city? I said, it was difficult, Bradford used to be a centre for the wool trade but was now struggling. He thanked me and told me I could leave.

Another time I was with my family in 2008 at the border between Canada and the United States as we were returning to Chicago from Toronto after attending my cousin's wedding there. I was with my wife, three young children, my mother and my grandfather's brother. Again, I was called for questioning.

'Please follow me sir.'

'Okay.' I turned towards my family and said I'd be back in a few minutes. I have in recent years prepared a plan of action in case of my arrest which I had informed my wife about and she knew what to do in the circumstances. I didn't trust the competence of the US immigration authorities. Again, I walked in to an office. A very young man was sitting at a desk behind a computer staring at my passport. He was flicking through it and shaking his head at the same time. He looked as if he had left high school a couple of years earlier. I thought to myself: 'Dumb down, he will not understand, don't be fooled by the uniform.' And sure enough, he seemed very fresh. 'How long have you lived in the UK, sir?'

'For about 30 years.'

'Are you sure?'

'Yes.' I realised, my passport was full of stamps from Arab countries. 'I lived in Jordan for about a year between 2002 and 2003.'

'Right. You've got a lot of visas here.'

'I was crossing borders to renew my visa in Jordan.'

'What do you do in the UK?' I had been asked this previously on entry into the US when again I had been pulled aside, I had answered 'I work in the national health service,' which didn't mean anything to the person asking the question.

'I work for the British government, I'm an advisor.'

He nodded. 'Who are you travelling with?' He was shaking his head. I think that he was thinking that how can I let this man pass when he has travelled so much?

'I'm travelling with my family.'

'Kids?'

'Yes.'

'How old are they?'

'Six, four and two.' It was about midnight on a Sunday night and we had already been waiting for about four hours.

He shook his head. I think that he was imagining what the kids would do to his office if he decided to detain me.

He waited a while. Shaking his head, 'Okay thank you sir, please wait outside.'

And that was it, a few minutes later they returned all our passports and told us that we were free to go. As I was waiting in the immigration centre, I remembered Martin Amis' request for Muslims to be harassed.

What were the important cultural moments?

The Bush years have had a huge effect upon our common culture in the US and here in Britain. That is to say that the politics of the time has not been ignored by the culture of its time, in fact one could say that there was a running cultural commentary on events; one that was not univocal though: it did represent different perspectives as the political arguments and positioning found their way into the screenplays of films and the output of leading writers. Sometimes, the cultural world waits, and reflects, and then comments through artistic production after the event. This was not the case during the Bush years.

It began with the attacks on 11th September itself. This terrorist attack was described on the day as 'like something from the movies'. But the commentary from the cultural quarter came not on the terrorist attack itself but upon the

US administration's response. The arguments about freedom of association, the permissibility of torture, the right to a fair trial – essentially the argument about the relation between politicians and the judiciary in a time of war dominated cultural responses to the Bush years. In Britain, there was also much agonising over the position of the Muslim community and how it was experiencing 'the war on terror'.

'24' – a spy thriller set in present-day America – began to air in the States in the autumn of 2001. It captured the *zeitgeist* and enthralled audiences while playing on their very real fears of an impending terrorist attack. The twists and turns, the unexpected, the double-crossings, the pressure of time – all served to make terrorists and the whole threat of terrorism look interesting and disturbing at the same time.[8] Its legitimation of torture, the ease with which suspects were tortured and killed, was unsettling. The BBC commissioned and then aired its own drama 'Dirty War' in September 2004 which depicted the aftermath of a dirty bomb attack on the city of London.[9] I remember one scene in this film which still shocks me as I recall it as this was the murder of a Muslim inmate by fellow prisoners. Shahid Aziz had been killed in Leeds Prison in the months prior to the screening of this programme. It was also shocking because it was a footnote to the major storyline, and was passed over as a detail in the bigger story. This was the nihilism of the Bush years. The BBC did also produce the documentary 'The Power of Nightmares' which focused on the climate of fear that the war on terror was generating and the series 'The State Within' which was a fictional story about a conspiracy within the American government to take the country to war.[10]

Channel 4 was to air 'Yasmin' written by Simon Beaufoy, 'Bradford Riots' directed by Neil Biswas, 'The Road to Guantanamo' directed by Michael Winterbottom and 'Britz' directed by Peter Kosminsky.[11] Theatre was not far behind. David Hare's 'Stuff Happens' and 'The Vertical Hour', Richard Norton-Taylor and Nicholas Kent's 'Justifying War', Victoria Britain and Gillian Slovo's 'Guantanamo' and David Edgar's 'Playing with Fire' were all staged during the Bush years.[12] Many of these television and theatre productions were important cultural events at the time receiving coverage and comment in the press.

The literary world also responded to the Bush years. Don De Lillo wrote 'Falling Man', Martin Amis wrote 'The Second Plane' and John Updike wrote 'Terrorist'.[13] 'Saturday' by Ian McEwan focused on the march against the Iraq war in 2003.[14] The film industry similarly responded to the themes thrown up by the Bush years. Ridley Scott directed 'Kingdom of Heaven', Michael Moore directed 'Fahrenheit 9/11' and critics noticed the influence of the Bush years on 'V for Vendetta', 'Star Wars Episode III: Revenge of the Sith' and 'The Dark Knight'.[15]

Much has been written or produced on 'the war on terror' and I don't want to provide an analysis of all of this but I would like to say that the cultural commentary has been consistent and mostly it has been critical of the dominant political narrative, some of the literary interventions excepted. However, though this cultural commentary has been critical of 'the war on terror', there have been fewer films, books or plays that have attempted to get inside the mind of a Muslim unless he happens to be a terrorist. There has therefore been plenty of criticism from a political position perspective but simultaneously cultural responses to the Bush years have in the main refrained from attempting to humanise or normalise a Muslim presence, this is while the domineering 'other-ising' discourse has continued to send out messages and stories that paint the Muslim community in stereotypical colours. This period has also seen very little cultural production from the Muslim community itself. Very few Muslim writers have been able to make it into the mainstream as cultural brokers for their communities. This has meant that although there may remain widespread agreement with the community on matters of policy such as torture, Guantanamo and the Iraq war, there remain real gaps in the understanding of Muslims and the Islamic faith. Muslims may need to step up to the plate on this issue to describe who they are and how they feel.

How do you think the Muslim community responded to this culturally?

The Muslim community's response in matters of culture has been fairly variegated. A new magazine was published in Britain: *Emel*, a Muslim lifestyle magazine. Probably the most famous Muslim artist in Britain is Mohammad Ali, a graffiti artist who combines street art with Islamic and political themes. Sami Yusuf has emerged as an immensely gifted singer. He has become very popular over the whole of the Muslim world. And there has been the emergence of Muslim comedians such as the 'Allah Made Me Funny' tour which includes Preacher Moss, Azhar Usman and Mo Amer. But it has probably been the genre of *nasheed*s that has proved to be the most developed and well-received. There are now countless *nasheed* artists, many with good voices but few with good songwriting abilities. Two that stand out here are Dawud Wharnsby-Ali and Kareem Salama. In many ways, it seems as if the Western Muslim community has responded to the Bush years through song. The literary side has been weak though: there are hardly any poems, plays, novels or short stories written as a response to 'the Bush years'. There is now the Muslim Writers Awards but this is still in the early stages of development and Muslim writing has a fair way to go to match the quality or popularity of Sami Yusuf. Most popular novels on the British Muslim experience have been written from an outsider perspective, for example Zadie Smith's 'White Teeth' or Monica Ali's 'Brick Lane'.[16] Muslim writers are emerging such as Yunus Alam, Zahid Hussain and Shelina Zahra Janmohamed but their voices have yet to have a wide impact on the Muslim community or British society itself.[17]

What do you think of Bush himself?

The arrival of Bush himself was an interesting moment. Many Muslims were angered by Bill Clinton because of the sanctions against Iraq and many Muslims in America had supported the Republicans in the 2000 elections as compassionate conservatives. The group of politicians around Bush were called neoconservatives after the movement that was based upon Leo Strauss' political philosophy. The neocons were described as political activists who wished to spread liberal democracy through force and that this was the justification for the Iraq war. This logic turned what began as a political war into a cultural war. A closer look at Leo Strauss' political philosophy revealed however that he was anti-liberal and his political philosophy was a conservative critique of liberalism. This was a strange discovery because it seemed that Leo Strauss was adopting a position that was fairly similar to a Muslim critique of modern society. And so it seemed that what was originally a political philosophy with which Muslims could engage and perhaps even partially agree was being used to justify a war that was being waged against Muslims. Unfortunately, very few people picked up on this and the problem of Muslims finding an intellectual location for themselves within a Western context remains. Bush's presidency came to be characterised by his personality, his group of advisors and a political philosophy that justified their ambitions. Bush himself was characterised as a buffoon, somebody whose job it was to read the autocues at press conferences and public speeches. The group of advisors were to provide the steel and substance to his presidency. They were the individuals of past administrative experience who could provide the strength to Bush's presidency that he needed. Bush will be remembered for his gaffes, a president who really should not have been president of the most powerful country on earth. He did not make his country proud and the world wondered what was so great about a political system that conjured up such an obviously inadequate candidate as president.

And Blair?

Blair is also a huge personality from the Bush years. He will be remembered for his ability to communicate, especially his speeches. He knew how to convince an audience, a country; he relied upon the trust that he asked for to win his arguments. But that was his downfall as well. It was an 'et tu Brute' moment when the country stared back in to his eyes and realised that he was in fact being economical with the truth on the most serious of matters. Blair will be remembered therefore for the enthusiasm, the hope and the trust that he inspired as well as the massive loss of trust that he generated after the Iraq war. He worried towards the end of his time as Prime Minister as to how history would judge him. I think history will judge him as someone who was not brave enough to stand up to the US administration in the lead up to the Iraq war. This could have been forgiven if he had then not gone on to become one of the great supporters of the invasion. History would have judged him differently if he had stood up at the time and spoken against the war on terror and the invasion of Iraq.

And Osama bin Laden?

The last 30 years could be described as the rise and fall of the Jihad movement. The Jihad movement has to be divided into three strands: the largest strand includes those engaged in freedom struggles for Muslims in minority situations such as Chechens in Russia, the Kashmiris in India and the Bosnians in Yugoslavia. The second strand consists of those Islamists who criticise more mainstream Islamist organisations for being too soft and argue that the Islamic state can only be achieved through violent means within Muslim countries and usually by waging a war against the government itself. Khalid Islambouli who assassinated Anwar Sadat may be considered to be from this strand. The third strand is those that have said that the war needs to be taken from Muslim countries to other countries that back the regimes in the Muslim world and specifically the United States. The Jihad movement was represented by these three strands but the second and third strand only really began to gather momentum in the seventies and then through the eighties as the third strand emerged as a dominant perspective in the nineties. Many of the individuals involved in the Jihad movement actually travelled through the three strands in their personal journeys. Osama bin Laden and Ayman Zawahiri can be seen as examples of this psychological trajectory. This was mainly because of the increasing desperation of the Jihad movement as it began to find that it had very few avenues left to achieve its ends. The attacks on 11th September though lead to two developments. The first is the actual tracking and assassination of jihadi leaders throughout the world. The destruction of their training camps in Afghanistan and breaking up of the financial support mechanisms that were in place. This had a practical, disruptive effect on the movement. A second development though and perhaps a much more important development was the turning of the tide of Muslim opinion against the Jihad movement. Until 11th September, there was a considerable amount of support for the Jihad movement in the Muslim world, and this was in the main because of their work in countries like Bosnia and Kashmir. However, if 11th September was the turning point, then further terrorist attacks and support and justification for them from jihadi leaders turned Muslims away from the Jihad movement. They now began to regard it as a corruption of Islamic teaching and perhaps also as a political miscalculation. Today, there is still considerable support to be found for Muslim communities that are experiencing difficulties because of their minority status however the other two strands are much weaker in their representation within the community compared to before.

The only group of people that have shown a level of support for terrorist groups like al-Qaeda now seem to be 'the newly practising'. These are people who seem to have become religious fairly quickly and internalised a radical, politicised identity version of the religion which incorporates a violent method of retribution as part of its understanding. They tend to mature out of it though as they begin to meet with scholars and develop a deeper understanding of their faith, something which is based upon the religious texts rather than a quick interpretation of media depictions of political situations involving Muslims throughout the world.

Who did badly in the Bush years within a British context?

When one begins to think about who did badly in the Bush years and who did well, then it is clear that of those on the national scene it was those who were able to provide some kind of consistent good judgment and political nous that came out as winners in the Bush years. Lord Nazir Ahmad was for example the *de facto* Minister for Muslim affairs in the first Blair term but his influence declined in the second term. This was because he was perhaps a bit too vociferous against the government of which he was a member. His political position was in effect right in my opinion i.e. that someone had to take a critical stance towards what the government was doing from 2002–2004, however his manner of execution was too abrasive and risky. Tariq Ramadan was also a voice that was poised to become an influential player in the Bush years but he has not been able to attract a mass following perhaps because his interventions have been too unfocused. Leadership during the Bush years was about providing leadership and guidance on specific issues and therefore depended upon outlining a response to specific developments. The Muslim Members of Parliament Muhammad Sarwar and Khalid Mahmood also lost ground during the Bush years. They were unable to articulate any vision for the Muslim community which the community could adopt and follow.

The Muslim Council of Britain has also emerged weaker from the Bush years. Their position prior to 9/11 was as Labour's only Muslim interlocutor. Word had it that Iqbal Sacranie, the Secretary-General of the MCB, had a direct line to Tony Blair. However, the influence of the MCB began to decline as the Bush years wore on. This is for two reasons. The first is the two wars in Afghanistan and Iraq. Ultimately, the MCB took a position against both wars (although it was slow to condemn the invasion of Afghanistan) and this included being part of a huge coalition against the invasion of Iraq. This soured relations between the MCB and the government. Secondly, and perhaps more importantly, the MCB was slow to respond to the needs of the government. From 9/11 onwards the government needed a partner with which it could work and upon which it could rely for the delivery of key policy objectives. The two key areas were community cohesion (or the integration debate) and counter-terrorism (and what later became the Prevent strand). On both agendas, the MCB didn't really respond in any way that could either be regarded as offering some form of direction to government or leadership to the Muslim community. If the government was frustrated before 7th July, the terrorist attacks of 2005 highlighted this great absence and the government effectively decided to instigate its own proto-Muslim leadership through the establishment of seven working groups themed around key policy areas. In one step, the MCB was sidelined and it was perhaps necessary at the time for a government whose priority was the safety of its citizens. Rival organisations such as the British Muslim Forum (headed by former Labour activist Khurshid Ahmad) and the Sufi Muslim Council (supported by former Labour activist Azhar Ali) were formed and these began to challenge the MCB on the national stage. In reality though, the MCB remains the main player because of its large number of affiliates and the other two organisations remain weak. The MCB's influence has however declined and with the advent of the Prevent strand in full measure across the country and the formation of the Young Muslim Advisory Group and the Muslim Women's Advisory Group by the British government's Department of Communities and Local Government, the MCB has been sidelined altogether. This could have been regarded as a price worth paying if the MCB had concomitantly strengthened its support within the Muslim community, but this hasn't happened either.

Other people whose influence has declined are the anti-Muslim extremists. Straight after 9/11 there was a great deal of interest in the anti-Muslim position, but, as the years have gone by, the positions of the anti-Muslim extremists have begun to appear more and more absurd as the solution they offer is further polarisation. Since the moderating tendency within the Muslim community has increased and become more vociferous during the Bush years, their position seems less accurate and therefore more paranoid. Their influence has certainly declined.

Who did well in the Bush years? Who came out as winners?

The Bush years have been very good for Muslim moderation. This was for two reasons: the first is the moral repugnance that many Muslims felt towards the terrorist attacks and their justifiers. This did genuinely move many Muslims to realise that we had a problem within the community. Secondly, Muslim moderation became a political necessity in response to terrorist attacks. Terrorist attacks led therefore to a strong revival of moderation simply because the opposing path was too politically fraught with danger. Those who therefore articulated a Muslim moderation with a clear and consistent approach emerged as winners from the Bush years. The Muslim community was seeking some direction and further polarisation was not a part of it so those leaders and spokespersons that articulated a moral response and political direction that exhibited some spine and some substance were those who were held in high regard. Sadiq Khan and Salma Yaqoob emerge here as two important voices that articulated this position very clearly.

One point that I'd like to add here though is that the Bush years were a very challenging time for people who were leading the Muslim community. The Bush years had a habit of throwing up scenarios that most people were not prepared for and probably had never thought about. Immediately, we, as a community, would be thrown into the eye of a major storm and we'd have all of three hours to respond with conviction and good judgement. This was asking a lot of most people and the first generation shied away from this responsibility, probably because they did not know how to respond. Many in the second generation stepped forward and I commend them for their bravery. Many have also made the occasional mistake. And this is where I think we should provide some breathing space for those who were brave enough to acknowledge the mistakes that they may have made during this period. Which brave soul is going to suggest that they could have done a better job? Perhaps, he who is without fear should cast the first stone, but I'm sorry to note that most people were afraid to stand up and be counted, but not too afraid to criticise. Having noted this, it should also be

said that internal criticism is a very useful corrective measure
if it's done in the right way. We need internal criticism, but we
need bravery and good judgement more.

Where do you think Quilliam Foundation fits into this?
I think the Quilliam Foundation has been a real disaster. This
is not because I disagree with their political position, as, in
essence, I agree with their political position. That is that we
have to question some of the influences upon British Muslims
and ensure that we help develop an approach that is conducive to
the preservation of Muslim identity as well as outreach towards
the wider community. The problem during the Bush years was
that internal critique (of aspects of the community) became
almost impossible during times of heightened politicisation.
The community was on the defensive though it had and has
many issues that it needs to face head on. We were coming from
a point of political oppositionalism and cultural isolation at the
same time. To help lead or navigate the community from this
point towards one in which the community is politically engaged
and culturally confidant is a delicate, sensitive process. There
were several Muslims who were leading this trend and it was
moving slowly but surely.

However, the Quilliam Foundation has almost totally
discredited this position not because of the position itself (or
what it means) but because of their tone and approach. The
community could be seen as a young teenager that was being
coaxed out of its teenage rage by a loving parent towards a
mature take on the world. The Quilliam Foundation instead
appeared as the angry parent who belittled the teenager and
moralised against him. The teenager at this point of course
walks out of the house. If the community does need some form
of leadership that seems very similar to a kind of paternalism,
then it should be a form of paternalism that helps the transition
and not one that confounds it.

I have been talking a lot about positionality and this is because the Bush years did in one sense foster a war of positioning

in the Muslim community. This can be seen time and again as major players such as government departments like the DCLG or think tanks like the Policy Exchange or commentators like Timothy Garton-Ash have spent much of the Bush years engaged in some exploratory anthropology-like exercise towards the Muslim community. Timothy Garton-Ash's search has been for a liberal Muslim who can be reconciled with his version of liberalism. He began by extolling the virtues of Ayaan Hirsi Ali as 'the new Voltaire', then moved on to Tariq Ramadan who works with him at Oxford University and is now acting as an advisor to the Quilliam Foundation.

What did you find shocking and unbelievable?

As I hinted earlier, the Bush years were one long surreal moment in which it seemed that anything could happen. This moment began with a terrorist attack that could have never been imagined and ended with the election of a young African-American President which was also previously unimaginable. The attacks in Madrid were unbelievable. The anti-war march in London on 15th February 2003 in which one million people marched was unbelievable. The invasion of Iraq was unbelievable. It was as if we were in some realm in which the impossible became possible. This is how it felt at the time, but a calmer voice within me urged me to resist 'the Bush years as exceptional' argument. There had been a previous Gulf War. The US had previously attacked Grenada. The Irish experience of internment was much worse than what the Muslim community experienced during the Bush years. So in many ways, the Bush years can be characterised by a series of unbelievable events, but it was also in many respects business as usual.

The other aspect of the Bush years that was genuinely shocking was the widening of the boundaries of acceptability in relation to what one could say about Muslims. 'Islam as an opportunistic infection in Europe', 'Muslims, like all dogs, share certain characteristics' and we should tame the Muslim community as we did during the Raj (I have paraphrased these quotes) have all been written by anti-Muslim spokespersons during these times.[18] That they passed without wider comment is shameful and that it remained for Muslims to question this language is also shocking. Reading material like this, I did feel at times that I couldn't believe that this was happening. These kinds of statements about any other community would have been regarded as unacceptable and condemned but they appear acceptable when ascribed to the Muslim community.

This makes me think that there were some that used the Bush years as an opportunity. I can think of two sectors here that had close but troubled relations with the Muslim community prior to the Bush years. The first is the race industry. Within the race industry there has been a variety of response. Commentators like Gary Younge of the *Guardian* and Karen Chouhan of the 1990 Trust have been at the forefront of support for the Muslim community whereas activists like Trevor Philips have used the Bush years to criticise the Muslim community for adopting a segregationist approach. His speech 'Sleepwalking to segregation' just after the 2005 attacks was probably one of the greatest acts of brinkmanship against the Muslim community in this period. The Anglican Church has been an institution that has developed relations with the community but this did not prevent leading members of the Church such as Bishop Michael Nazir-Ali from criticising the Muslim community through arguments that again presented the community as a problem, seeking to isolate itself and refusing to engage. There certainly was some opportunism during this period and it was revealing as to the true intentions of those who previously had painted themselves as friends of the Muslim community.

What has changed and what will be the long-term impact of the Bush years?

Thinking about the Bush years I am taken back to the Rushdie Affair. The main event was the issuing of the fatwa by Ayatollah Khomeini against Salman Rushdie on 15th February 1989. The book burning that is associated with the fatwa is something which gathered significance retrospectively. At the time (early January 1989), it didn't receive that much coverage in the press. The Rushdie Affair though has been described as the origin of the 'Islam problem'. Some commentators have attempted to force this narrative. For example Kenan Malik has titled his new book 'From Fatwa to Jihad' as if there is some clear link between the two.[19] There may be, but only in the minds of those who wish to construct a powerful anti-Muslim prejudice that preys upon the deepest fears of an already fearful Western population. The Rushdie Affair can't really be described as the origin of the 'Islam problem'. The *halal* meat episode and the Honeyford Affair are perhaps important first experiences of the tensions around multiculturalism but the war in Bosnia was the formative event in the development of the more radical trends in British Islam rather than the Rushdie Affair. 'From Bosnia to Jihad' would be a more credible account of the narrative and it makes much more sense: the Jihad movement gained strength directly because of the weakness that many Muslims felt as a result of the murder and rape in Bosnia.

The Rushdie Affair at the time though seemed to last forever and many of us who were there then felt that it was a really bad period to live through. However, as in the Sufi understanding, reality may contradict appearances. The Rushdie Affair became a time of great soul-searching within the community and considerable discussion as to its future. Out of the Rushdie Affair there emerged an approach towards understanding Muslim identity that was strident and yet focused on the naturalisation of a Muslim presence within Britain. Many people discovered themselves as Muslims thereafter and found ways to contribute towards such a natural Muslim presence within Britain.

The Bush years I think will have the same kind of effect and in fact I have already seen it happening. There is a large proportion of the third generation that is now politically focused, aware and strident. The difference between now and then is that then – 20 years ago – many of us had to make do with poor resources, many questions were left unanswered and we had very little means to figure out what we were going to do next. This is no longer the case. In publishing, the books that are available now are an amazing source of information and guidance. In terms of lecture series, there are many, many educational products available for Muslim young people which can help them through faith spiritually, intellectually and practically. These services rendered by leaders like Sheikh Hamza Yusuf, Dr Umar Abdallah, Sheikh Zaid Shakir and Sheikh Abdal Hakim Murad are a great service to the Muslim community and have been incredibly helpful. The internet through Youtube and e-mail contact and online shops also makes all of these resources instantly accessible. The facilities and resources are therefore great and I sometimes marvel at the lack of appreciation from some 18 year olds that I have come across for the resources that they have available and that we never had then.

The other main difference between now and then is that the move in the nineties was towards cultural isolation and political oppositionalism. The move today is towards cultural and political engagement. The politicisation of the Bush years has therefore rapidly speeded up the development of a Muslim identity in Britain and the West in general and it has done so by politicising Muslim youth, that is marking their identity, which has then forced them to explore this identity through a much wider variety and better quality of resources that are now available and in the direction of engagement. This means that today and henceforth there is a much greater presence in the public sphere than before. That is to say, that where the doors have been opened such as in the *Guardian*'s comment pages, then there is a sizeable Muslim presence that is seeking to respond to the various challenges that we face and where the doors have been closed such as in the *Telegraph*'s comment pages, then Muslims are few and far between. One example of this shift from protest towards engagement is the Muslim student body FOSIS, the Federation of Student Islamic Societies. The nineties were a time in which FOSIS was either excluded from the deliberations of the National Union of Students or engaged in some antagonistic altercation with the NUS. Today, FOSIS representatives have been elected on to the national NUS body and there are in the main strong and mutually beneficial and constructive relations between the NUS and FOSIS. In this sense, one could say that Muslim politics is maturing.

The other point that I would like to add here is that I think that we can now begin to see the shoots of a new stage of development for the community: institutionalization. If the first three stages were mosque building, identity politics and now engagement, then hopefully the community is currently moving towards embedding itself as individuals and communities throughout British society. Bruce Tuckman came up with a four-stage model of group development: forming, storming, norming and performing.[20] The first few decades of post-war Muslim life in Britain could be described as a mixture of storming and forming. It seems that we are beginning to witness the first examples of norming behaviour as Muslims begin to establish themselves throughout British society. This move towards institutionalization however is dependent upon the kind of social capital that will become available to the community. It is clear that much of the social capital that already exists within the community is ethnic-based, and that there is also unfortunately in my view a retrograde counter-development towards ethnic chauvinism – i.e. the renewal of ethnic and cultural identities that are very specific to certain regions of South Asia. However, the move towards a religious identification is an attempt to maintain links with history while not being bound by parochial boundaries. This is leading to the emergence of two ways of thinking towards cultural and religious identities: the unifiers and the dividers. The unifiers are attempting to construct narratives of inclusion across ethnicities and even religions, while the dividers are attempting to construct narratives of particularity for their specific ethnicities. This is a worrying development and seems to be about the reproduction of certain ethnic privileges.

If there are several layers of representation: academic (e.g. university professors), media (e.g. journalists and commentators), policy (policy wonks and civil servants) and political (members of the House of Commons and the House of Lords) and the representation has been continuous and intense then the story of engagement is very far from complete. There were only eight Muslim Members of the House of Commons in 2010, and the contributions of the Muslim members of the House of Lords have been lacklustre compared to other Peers. There are very few national Muslim commentators and also very few professors in the human, social and political sciences. But the numbers are slowly increasing.

The extent to which this period has had a transformative effect upon the community can be envisaged by the changes that have occurred to some its leading individuals. Sadiq Khan began this period as a lawyer working with Louise Christian on cases that were taking the government to task on its counter-terrorism strategy. Sadiq Khan then became an MP and then a Minister for the Department of Communities and Local Government which leads on race equality and cohesion matters. Salma Yaqoob was transformed through her experience of anti-Muslim prejudice and has since become a leading political voice for the community, appearing on national television and speaking in front of thousands on numerous occasions. Maajid Nawaz began this period as a leading member of Hizb ut-Tahrir. He was arrested in Egypt and jailed for being a part of Hizb ut-Tahrir. He was released, returned to Britain and began to appear on satellite Muslim television and then announced his departure from Hizb ut-Tahrir to lead a counter-extremism think tank that is heavily backed by government.

It's still too early to tell what all of this will lead to and this is probably why we are currently engaged in a war of positioning and have been so since 9/11. What is clear though is that where there is under-representation of Muslims in public life, it's not because of a lack of ambition or aspiration or even talent, it is instead due to the fact that the doors through which one has to enter in order to gain a foothold in any of these arenas are firmly shut.

There has been real resistance from policymakers and commentators to respond to the terrorism question simply as a political issue and there has instead been a real readiness to move towards defining the problem as a cultural problem and so policymakers and commentators have lead on the war of positioning by putting forward the examples of Ed Husain and Anjem Choudary as leaders for the community to contend with. Salma Yaqoob, Inayat Bunglawala and others have also fought to carve out a political position that retains some critical edge while remaining integrationist in principle. That Ed Husain has been actively supported by the government and Anjem Choudary is given instant access to the mainstream media – something which is almost unimaginable for most intelligent, articulate, sound, decent and generally persuasive Muslims – shows that the matter of the future of Muslim identity is actively being contested by several actors. At the heart of this is a process that seems to be repeating itself and that I would like to term the 'coconut–extremist dialectic'. First of all, a word or two on coconuts and extremists. Most people are presumably familiar with the identity characterisation of extremists. It is a lay conception which if disputed remains well-understood. 'Coconuts' is a pejorative term describing those that have opted for social mobility while simultaneously abandoning their cultural and religious heritage. They are brown on the outside, white on the inside.

There seems to be a process at play which has repeated itself across a wide variety of situations, most specifically in the media but this also applies to cultural matters in general. The process is as follows. A coconut for a wide variety of reasons decides to leave his community and adopts a position of criticism and rejection of his background. He enters the world of journalism on the back of this critique, makes it clear that this is his stance and attempts to make himself accepted as somebody without such a background i.e. on his own terms. The pathways to achievement are open to him and success is relatively more attainable. However, the coconuts then face an obstacle in that their employers persist in viewing them as ethnic representatives. This takes a rather comical turn when these same coconuts are asked to return to their communities to provide some analysis on these same communities for the wider public. They are then seen returning to their old families and friends while asking for some kind of access to the people and issues that matter. It also introduces a conflict of interest into the equation as their personal life trajectories (and presumably emotions) are tied deeply to the object of study. This whole process also confounds the whole nature of cross-cultural understanding. It is in the interests of the coconuts that the extremists are forever presented as unreasonable. The day that the extremist alternative is legitimated is the same day that the coconut option looses its credibility, that is, once the extremists are accepted the coconuts will look silly standing alone on Mount White Elephant. I am not interested in denigrating people who have chosen alternative ways of living, but I do find it difficult that my path towards inclusion – metaphorically speaking – is perpetually problematized by those who have an irredeemable conflict of interest. This process needs to be examined, and extremists or should we say 'practising Muslims' should be given a chance to present themselves on their own terms.

On the point of inclusion, I should also mention a couple of incidents that made me laugh after the event but which nevertheless describe the politicised nature of this whole process. The sociologist Erving Goffman speaks of the point at which the actor moves from backstage to front stage as an important point to pick up on the subtleties of the whole process.[21] I have attempted moves towards inclusion (i.e. from backstage to front stage) on numerous occasions. On one such occasion, I had been attending an academic seminar for quite a while but had never spoken. One day I decided to muster up some courage to make my point which was on social constructionism (i.e. that people live within their own worlds of understanding). I was immediately responded to by a colleague who suggested that I believed in the worldwide Jewish conspiracy. I was completely shocked by his intervention and unfortunately did not have sufficient wit about me to respond. Another time, I managed to gain access to a policy wonk meeting. As I was doing the rounds at the end, one Asian non-Muslim organiser came up to me and made an anti-Semitic joke (again about Jewish supremacy) and then laughed. I kept a straight face and politely explained why

173

her opinion was wrong. No doubt, if out of politeness, I had nervously laughed along, I would have been termed an anti-Semite thereafter. Both incidences reveal the tense nature of incorporation and the prejudices involved.

These are merely a couple of examples from my own personal experience, but the rhetorical pushing away (including using other forms of assumed prejudice on my part) as I have attempted to include myself has been an all-too-familiar experience in my personal struggle to ensure that I am included and involved in a matter that affects me. I have remained persistent and patient. Unfortunately, others decide that it is better to give up on attempting to integrate, they argue, and up to a point, I agree with them that they cannot integrate themselves, they can only be integrated. Muslims are at present under-represented in all areas of public life. A transition towards a more equitable outcome will require an understanding of why the situation is as it is today.

Endnotes

Introduction

1. Clifford Geertz, 'Which Way to Mecca?' *New York Review of Books*, 12th June 2003.
2. Denise Jodelet, *Madness and Social Representations*, ed. G. Duveen, trans. T. Pownell (Hemel Hempstead: Harvester Wheatsheaf, 1991).
3. Charles Husband, 'The Political Context of Muslim Communities' Participation in British Society', in B. Lewis and D. Schnapper (eds.), *Muslims in Europe* (London: Pinter, 1994), p.80.
4. William Montgomery Watt, *Muslim-Christian Encounters: Perceptions and Misperceptions* (London: Routledge, 1991).
5. Edward Said, *Orientalism* (London: Penguin, 1978).
6. Alain Grosrichard, *The Sultan's Court: European Fantasies of the East*, trans. L. Heron (London: Verso, 1998). The book takes the specific example of Montesquieu, and notes that others like Voltaire had an alternative opinion.
7. M. Dolar, 'Introduction: The Subject Supposed to Enjoy' in A. Grosrichard, *The Sultan's Court: European Fantasies of the East* (London: Verso, 1998), p.xi.
8. Bryan Turner, *Orientalism, Postmodernism and Globalism*. (London: Routledge, 1994), p.39.
9. Kathryn Woodward, Concepts of Identity and Difference, in Kathryn Woodward (ed.), *Identity and Difference*, (London: Sage, 1997), p.18.
10. Mohja Kahf, *Western Representations of the Muslim Woman* (Austin, Texas: University of Texas Press, 1999).
11. S.M. Atif Imtiaz, 'Identity and the Politics of Representation: The Case of Muslim Youth in Bradford', Ph.D. Thesis (University of London, 2002).

12 For other examples of research into the history of Western views of Islam see Richard Southern, *Western Views of Islam in the Middle Ages* (Cambridge, MA: Harvard, 1962); Ahmad Gunny, *Images of Islam in Eighteenth-Century Writings* (London: Grey Seal, 1996); Norman Daniel, *Islam and the West* (Oxford: OneWorld, 1993); Rana Kabbani, *Europe's Myths of the Orient* (London: Macmillan, 1986).

13 For further reading, please consult: Gertrude Himmelfarb, *The Demoralisation of Society: From Victorian Values to Modern Values* (London: The Institute of Economic Affairs Health and Welfare Unit, 1995); David Utting (ed.), *Contemporary Social Evils* (Bristol: Joseph Rowntree Foundation, 2009); Ralph Fevre, *The Demoralisation of Western Culture: Social Theory and the Dilemmas of Modern Living* (London: Continuum, 2000); John Gray, *Enlightenment's Wake: Politics and Culture at the Close of the Modern Age* (London: Routledge, 1995); Paul Heelas, Scott Lash and Paul Morris (eds.), *Detraditionalisation: Critical Reflections on Authority and Identity* (Oxford: Blackwell, 1996).

14 Alasdair MacIntyre explores this further in *After Virtue: A Study in Moral Theory* (London: Duckworth, 1985).

Chapter 1

1 This essay was written in the immediate aftermath of September 11. It remains unedited and so is an honest account of one person's response to the terrorist attacks and the debate that followed.

2 Sigmund Freud, *The Standard Edition of the Complete Psychological Works of Sigmund Freud*, trans. J. Strachey, 24 vols (London: Hogarth. 1953-1974), 14:275.

3 There is some disagreement as to the exact number of victims. The BBC in the immediate aftermath suggested that up to 50,000 could have died. However, Michael Ellison writing in the *Guardian* (28th October 2001) quoted New York City officials as putting the figure at 4964. The *New York Times* suggested 2950; the *USA Today* proposed 2680; the Associated Press 2625; and the American Red Cross which had received $500 million in donations towards supporting the families of the deceased suggested 2563. Why is it that if I were to say that there is no independent confirmation of these figures, replicating the BBC's response to casualty figures from Afghanistan, I feel that I am somehow less of a human being?

4 In attempting to explain how the Holocaust could have happened, social psychological studies into the nature of fascism suggested that

the authoritarian personality forced the silent masses into submission cf. Theodor Adorno et al, *The Authoritarian Personality* (New York: Harper and Row, 1950). Any such examination today would have to include the role of the media as an agent for comatisation.

5   Both papers can be found in: Azzam Tamimi, *Power-Sharing Islam?* (London: Liberty for Muslim World Publications, 1993).

6   For further reading: François Burgat and William Dowell, *The Islamic Movement in North Africa* (Austin, Texas: University of Texas Press, 1993).

7   But what about Kosovo? How can a Muslim explain the bombing of Yugoslavia by the US and Britain in order to protect a Muslim population? It certainly confounded expectations, and experience, and that is why Islamists remain mute on this issue. It remains as one example against a whole list of counter-examples. International politics and Popperian falsificationism simply don't add up.

8   Tariq Ali and Howard Brenton, *Iranian Nights*, Channel 4, 20th May 1989.

9   The consequence of a denotation of barbarism is the civilising process which requires political control and military action.

10   Quoted on *The Late Show*, BBC2, 8th May 1989.

11   *Guardian*, 5th November 1997.

12   Karl Mannheim, *Ideology and Utopia*, Edward Shils (trans.) (London: Routledge and Kegan Paul, 1972), p.43.

13   Gustav Ichheiser, 'Misunderstandings in Human Relations: A Study in False Social Perception', *American Journal of Sociology*, 55 (suppl.), (1949).

14   For examples of how seemingly liberal ideas can be used towards illiberal ends see: Bhikhu Parekh, 'Decolonising Liberalism', in Jan Nederveen Pieterse and Bhikhu Parekh (eds.), *Decolonising the Imagination* (London: Zed Press, 1993); Edward Said, *Culture and Imperialism* (London: Vintage, 1993); Margaret Wetherell and Jonathan Potter, *Mapping the Language of Racism* (Hemel Hempstead: Harvester/Wheatsheaf, 1992).

15   Jan Nederveen Pieterse, *White on Black: Images of Africa and Blacks in Western Popular Culture* (London: Yale University Press, 1992).

16   For further reading: W. Pereira, *Inhuman Rights: The Western System and Global Human Rights Abuse* (New York: Apex Press. 1997).

17   Susan George, *Feeding the Few* (Washington: Institute for Policy Studies, 1979); Susan George, *A Fate Worse than Debt* (Harmondsworth: Penguin, 1988); Vandana Shiva, *Biopiracy* (Cambridge, MA:

South End Press, 1997); Vandana Shiva, *Stolen Harvest* (Cambridge, MA: South End Press, 1999).

18 John Locke, *Two Treatises of Government* (London: J.M. Dent and Sons, 1989/1690), p.140.

19 Bobby Sayyid, *A Fundamental Fear: Eurocentrism and the Emergence of Islamism* (London: Zed Books. 1997), p.118. See also a Jewish attempt to provide common ground between internal critics of the West and those of religious faith: Jonathan Sacks, *The Persistence of Faith: Religion, Morality and Society in a Secular Age* (London: Weidenfeld and Nicholson, 1991).

20 Anthony Giddens, *Beyond Left and Right* (Cambridge: Polity Press, 1994).

21 Brendan Simms, *Unfinest Hour: How Britain Helped to Destroy Bosnia* (London: Penguin Press, 2001).

22 Samantha Power, 'Bystanders to Genocide', *Atlantic Monthly*, September 2001.

23 Jean Baudrillard, *The Gulf War Did Not Take Place* (Sydney: Power Publications, 1995).

24 Gordon Allport, *The Nature of Prejudice* (New York: Doubleday Anchor, 1954).

25 *Sunday Times*, 7th October 2001.

26 *Independent on Sunday*, 18th November 2001.

27 Roxanne Euben, *Enemy in the Mirror: Islamic Fundamentalism and the Limits of Modern Rationalism* (Princeton, NJ: Princeton University Press, 1999).

28 'Sociology suggests that you cannot have modernisation, technology, urbanisation and bureaucratisation without the cultural baggage that goes with it and this baggage is essentially a post-Enlightenment system of thought'. Bryan Turner, *Orientalism, Postmodernism and Globalism* (London: Routledge, 1994), p.8.

29 For further reading: Chalmers Johnson, *Blowback: The Costs and Consequences of American Empire* (New York: Henry Holt and Company, 2000).

30 *Observer*, 14th October 2001.

31 *Guardian*, 6th October 2001.

32 *Observer*, 14th October 2001.

33 The *Telegraph* published an Islam supplement on Thursday 15th November 2001, presumably to counter the misconceptions that other papers were spreading.

34 Bobby Sayyid, *A Fundamental Fear*.

35 Zadie Smith, *White Teeth* (Harmondsworth: Penguin, 2000), p.434.

36 Minorities have been found to appear in the news as individuals in stereotypical roles (criminals, rioters) or as members of controversial organisations; see Teun Van Dijk, *Racism and the Press* (London: Routledge, 1991), p.85.

37 Edward Said, *Covering Islam* (London: Vintage, 1997).

38 Alain Grosrichard, *The Sultan's Court: European Fantasies of the East* (London: Verso, 1998), p.34-5.

39 Gustav Ichheiser, 'Sociopsychological and Cultural Factors in Race Relations', *American Journal of Sociology*, 54 (1949); 395-9.

40 Edward Said, *Orientalism: Western Conceptions of the Orient* (Harmondsworth: Penguin, 1995).

41 Diana Rose, 'Representations of Madness on British Television: A Social Psychological Analysis', Ph.D. Thesis (University of London, United Kingdom, 1996).

42 Akbar Ahmed, *Postmodernism and Islam: Predicament and Promise* (London: Routledge, 1992); Ziauddin Sardar, *Postmodernism and the Other: The New Imperialism of Western Culture* (London: Pluto Press, 1998); Bobby Sayyid, *A Fundamental Fear.*

43 *Express on Sunday*, 11th November 2001.

44 *Guardian*, 3rd November 2001.

45 Herman Ouseley, *Community Pride not Prejudice: Making Diversity Work in Bradford* (Bradford: Bradford Race Review, 2001).

46 *Observer*, 30th September 2001.

47 Herman Ouseley, *Community Pride not Prejudice*, 2.5.1, 2.5.5 and 2.5.10.

48 *Guardian*, 28th September 2001.

49 'The logic of Islamism is threatening because it fails to recognise the universalism of the western project', Bobby Sayyid, *A Fundamental Fear*, p.129.

50 Albert Camus, *Notebooks 1942-1951*, J. O'Brien (trans.) (New York: Modern Library, 1965), p.23.

Chapter 2

1 For good discussions on the media's influence on the distribution of information, read Neil Postman, *Amusing Ourselves to Death* (London: Penguin, 2005) and John Thompson, *Ideology and Modern Culture* (Cambridge: Polity Press, 1990).

2   Bhikhu Parekh, 'Why Terror?', *Prospect*, April 2004.

3   Jan Nederveen Pieterse, *White on Black: Images of Africa and Blacks in Western Popular Culture* (London: Yale University Press, 1992).

4   See for example his contribution to the multiculturalism debate in Sander Gilman, '"Barbaric" Rituals', in Susan Okin (ed.), *Is Multiculturalism Bad for Women?* (Princeton: Princeton University Press, 1999).

5   This criticism of Muslim practice makes no distinction between that practice which is obligated, permitted, disliked or forbidden in Islamic law. It similarly makes no distinction between those practices which are geographically confined to certain cultures and those which are universal Muslim practices (like the obligation to give charity).

6   Bhikhu Parekh, *Rethinking Multiculturalism* (London: Palgrave Macmillan, 2006), p.198.

7   Ernest Gellner, *Postmodernism, Reason and Religion* (London: Routledge, 1992).

8   Clifford Geertz, *Islam Observed* (Chicago: University of Chicago Press, 1968), p.54.

9   William James, *The Varieties of Religious Experience* (Harmondsworth: Penguin, 1982) p.38.

10   For an exposition of Islamic psychology, see Imam al-Ghazali's *Disciplining the Soul* (Cambridge: Islamic Texts Society, 1995).

11   Iris Marion Young, *Justice and the Politics of Difference* (Princeton: Princeton University Press, 1990).

12   This distinction between an 'inside Islam' and an 'outside Islam' concerns the psychology of a person more than his behaviour. Two people may behave the same in terms of level of activity, but psychologically, one may be with His Lord, and the second may be with society, that is, the news reports.

13   For good expositions of Islamic *adab* see Ibn al-Husayn al-Sulami, *The Way of Sufi Chivalry* (Vermont: Inner Traditions International, 1991) and Abdul Fattah Abu Ghudda, *Islamic Manners,* Muhammad Zahid Abu Ghudda (trans.), S. M. Hasan al Banna (ed.) (Swansea: Awakening Publications, 2001).

14   For example, see Nuh Keller, 'Why Muslims follow Madhhabs?' (1995, http://www.masud.co.uk/ISLAM/nuh/madhhabstlk.htm, accessed 13th September 2009) and A. H. Murad, *Understanding the Four Madhhabs: the facts about ijtihad and taqlid* (Cambridge: Muslim Academic Trust, 1999), also available at http://www.masud. co.uk/ISLAM/ahm/newmadhh.htm.

15 For a clear exposition of this position see: M.A. Al-Akiti, 'Defending the Transgressed by Censuring the Reckless against the Killing of Civilians', in A. Malik (ed.) *The State We're In: Identity, Terror and the Law of Jihad* (Bristol: Amal Press, 2006); also available at http://www.warda.info/fatwa.pdf.

16 See *al-'Asr* 103:3.

17 Iqbal Sacranie, 'Secretary General's Speech', Muslim Council of Britain's Annual General Meeting, 4th June 2006, pp. 16-17, available at http://www.mcb.org.uk/uploads/SECGEN.pdf.

18 Tariq Modood, 'Remaking Multiculturalism after 7/7' (2005), http://opendemocracy.net/conflict-terrorism/multiculturalism_2879.jsp.

19 T. Modood, *Multiculturalism: A Civic Idea* (Cambridge: Polity Press, 2007).

20 For more on the relationship between law and culture see: Lawrence Rosen, *The Justice of Islam* (Oxford: Oxford University Press, 2000).

Chapter 5

1 Quoted from the poem 'My Wine' by Sheikh 'Abd al-Rahman al-Shaghuri, translated by Muhammad Isa Waley.

2 See Charles Le Gai Eaton, *Remembering God* (Cambridge: Islamic Texts Society, 2001).

3 Martin Lings, *What is Sufism?* (Cambridge: Islamic Texts Society, 1993).

4 For a good history of the social sciences, see Peter Manicas, *A History and Philosophy of the Social Sciences* (Oxford: Blackwell, 1987).

Chapter 6

1 Margaret Wetherell, Michelyn Lafleche and Robert Berkeley (eds.), *Identity, Ethnic Diversity and Community Cohesion* (London: Sage, 2007); Tariq Modood, *Multiculturalism: A Civic Idea* (Cambidge: Polity Press, 2007); Anne Phillips, *Multiculturalism without Culture* (Princeton: Princeton University Press, 2007); Keith Banting and Will Kymlicka (eds.), *Multiculturalism and the Welfare State* (Oxford: Oxford University Press, 2006).

2 Margaret Thatcher made this statement in an interview with *Women's Own* magazine, 31st October 1987.

3 David Cameron made this statement in his victory speech on 6th December 2005 for the leadership election contest of the Conservative Party.

4   Peter Scott, Christopher Baker and Elaine Graham (eds.), *Remoralising Britain: Political, Ethical and Theological Perspectives of New Labour* (London: Continuum, 2009).

5   Francis Davis, Elizabeth Paulhus and Andrew Bradstock, *Moral, but no Compass: Government, Church and the Future of Welfare* (Cambridge: Von Hugel Institute, 2008).

6   Reena Bhavnani, Heidi Mirza and Veena Meetoo, *Tackling the Roots of Racism* (Bristol: Policy Press, 2005).

7   Herman Ouseley, *Community Pride not Prejudice: Making Diversity Work in Bradford* (Bradford: Bradford Race Review, 2001).

8   Ted Cantle, *A Report of the Independent Review Team* (London: Home Office, 2001).

9   Henry Tam, 'The Case for Progressive Solidarity', in Wetherall, Lafleche and Berkeley (eds.), p.21.

10   Ibid. p. 21.

11   Trevor Phillips, 'After 7/7, Sleepwalking to Segregation', speech at Manchester Town Hall, 22nd September 2005.

12   Susan Okin, *Is Multiculturalism Bad for Women?* (Princeton: Princeton University Press, 1999).

13   Phillips, *Multiculturalism without Culture*, p.8.

14   John Gray, *Two Faces of Liberalism* (Cambridge: Polity Press: 2002).

15   David Goodhart, 'Too Diverse', *Prospect*, February 2004.

16   Keith Banting, Richard Johnston, Will Kymlicka and Stuart Soroka, 'Do Multicultural Policies Erode the Welfare State? An Empirical Analysis', in Banting and Kymlicka (eds.), p.83.

17   Geoffrey Evans, 'Is Multiculturalism Eroding Support for Welfare Provision? The British Case', in Banting and Kymlicka (eds.).

18   Peter Kraus and Karen Schonwalder, 'Multiculturalism in Germany: Rhetoric, Scattered Experiments and Future Chances', in Banting and Kymlicka (eds.).

19   David Miller, 'Multiculturalism and the Welfare State: Theoretical Reflections', in Banting and Kymlicka (eds.).

20   Miller, 'Multiculturalism and the Welfare State', p.338.

21   John Myles and Sebastien St-Arnaud, 'Population Diversity, Multiculturalism and the Welfare State: Should Welfare State Theory be Revised?' in Banting and Kymlicka (eds.).

22   For example, see the section on the future of adult social care, http://www.jrf.org.uk/work/workarea/future-of-adult-social-care.

Chapter 7

[1] 'Helping Our Elders' is a fictional charity that has been commissioned by a Metropolitan Council serving a diverse community in order to help social services reach an ageing South Asian population. It has bilingual workers and considers the spiritual and cultural needs of its service users.

[2] For one examination of this issue see Serge Moscovici, *Society against Nature: The Emergence of Human Societies*, Sasha Rabinovitch (trans.) (London: The Hogarth Press, 1976).

[3] *Our Health, Our Care, Our Say* (London: Department of Health, 2006).

[4] Ibid.

[5] Ibid.

[6] Tariq Modood, 'Multiculturalism's Civic Future: A Response' (2007), http://opendemocracy.net/faith_ideas/europe_islam/multicultural-ism_future, accessed 13th September 2009).

[7] Friedrich Nietzsche, *Beyond Good and Evil*, Marion Faber (trans. and ed.), (Oxford: Oxford University Press, 1998), p.115.

Chapter 9

[1] With apologies to William Wordsworth.

[2] For further reading: François Burgat. and William Dowell, *The Islamic Movement in North Africa* (Austin, Texas: University of Texas Press. 1993).

[3] Office for Security and Counter-terrorism, Statistics on Terrorism Arrests, (2009), http://security.homeofiice.gov.uk/news-publications/news-speeches/stats-terrorism-arrests, accessed 13th September 2009).

[4] See Khalida Khan, *Preventing Violent Extremism and the Prevent Strategy – A Muslim Response* (London: An-Nisa Society, 2009); Arun Kundnani, *Spooked: How not to Prevent Violent Extremism* (London: Institute of Race Relations, 2009); House of Commons – Communities and Local Government Committee, *Preventing Violent Extremism* (London: The Stationery Office, 2010).

[5] *Guardian*, 13th July 2010.

[6] The website for the Muslim Public Affairs Committee UK can be found at www.mpacuk.org.

[7] See Michael Ignatieff, *The Lesser Evil: Political Ethics in an Age of Terror* (Princeton: Princeton University Press, 2004); and Alan

Dershowitz, 'Want to Torture? Get a Warrant', *San Francisco Chronicle*, 22nd January 2002.

8   *24*, Fox, aired on BBC2, 2001-2002.

9   *Dirty War*, BBC1, 26th September 2004.

10   *The State Within*, BBC1, November-December 2006.

11   *Yasmin*, Channel 4, 13th January 2005; *Bradford Riots*, Channel 4, 4th May 2006; *The Road to Guantanamo*, directed Michael Winterbottom (Channel 4, 2006); *Britz*, Channel 4, 31st October–1st November 2007.

12   David Hare, *Stuff Happens*, 2004; David Hare, *The Vertical Hour*, 2006; Richard Norton-Taylor and Nicholas Kent, *Justifying War*, 2003; Victoria Britain and Gillian Slovo, *Guantanamo*, 2005; David Edgar, *Playing with Fire*, 2005.

13   Don De Lillo, *Falling Man* (London: Picador, 2008); Martin Amis, *The Second Plane: September 11, Terror and Boredom* (New York: Knopf Publishing, 2008); John Updike, *The Terrorist* (London: Penguin, 2007).

14   Ian McEwan, *Saturday* (London: Vintage, 2006).

15   *Kingdom of Heaven* (Twentieth Century Fox, 2005), Ridley Scott (dir.); *Fahrenheit 9/11* (Fellowship Adventure Group, 2004), Michael Moore (dir.); *V for Vendetta* (Silver Pictures, 2006), James McTeigue (dir.); *Star Wars Episode III: Revenge of the Sith* (Lucasfilm, 2005), George Lucas (dir.); *The Dark Knight* (Warner Bros, 2008), Christopher Nolan (dir.).

16   Zadie Smith, *White Teeth* (London: Penguin, 2001); Monica Ali, *Brick Lane* (London: Doubleday, 2003).

17   Yunus Alam, *Kilo* (Wakefield: Route, 2002); Zahid Hussain, *Curry Mile* (Suitcase, 2006); Shelina Jan Mohamed, *Love in a Headscarf* (London: Aurum Press, 2009).

18   Douglas Murray, 'What are we to do about Islam?', Pym Fortuyn Memorial Conference, Sunday 19th February 2006; Will Cummins, 'Muslims are a Threat to our Way of Life', *Telegraph*, 25th July 2004; Melanie Phillips, 'Sleepwalking into Islamisation', *Daily Mail*, 8th July 2008.

19   Kenan Malik, *From Fatwa to Jihad: The Rushdie Affair and its Legacy* (London: Atlantic Books, 2009).

20   Tuckman, Bruce, 'Developmental Sequence in Small Groups', *Psychological Bulletin* 63 (6), (1965):384-99.

21   Erving Goffman, *The Presentation of Self in Everyday Life* (New York: Doubleday Anchor, 1959).